ISBN 978-0-483-59806-5
PIBN 10790762

This book is a reproduction of an important historical work. Forgotten Books uses state-of-the-art technology to digitally reconstruct the work, preserving the original format whilst repairing imperfections present in the aged copy. In rare cases, an imperfection in the original, such as a blemish or missing page, may be replicated in our edition. We do, however, repair the vast majority of imperfections successfully; any imperfections that remain are intentionally left to preserve the state of such historical works.

RECOGNITION

OF

THE CREATOR

IN DAILY LIFE.

BY THE COMPILER OF "INSTAURATIO."

Mrs. N. S. Sperry.

"My people habe forgotten me days without number."

HARTFORD:

PRESS OF CASE, LOCKWOOD & BRAINARD.

1873.

THE NEW YEAR.

1. *Now they began on the first day of the first month to sanctify.*

'It is a merciful provision that the Stream of Time does not run in one continuous flow, but it is taken up and separated into portions which are for ' signs and for seasons, and for days and years.' These changes and vicissitudes present us successively with renewed occasions and encouragements to amend our lives, and to set out as it were on a new course.'

> ' Pure and bright it lies before us,
>   Like the snowy moor untrod '—

> The future hides in it   And solemn before us
> Gladness and sorrow;   Veiled the dark Portal,
> We press still thorow;   Goal of all mortal;—
> Nought that abides in it   Stars silent rest o'er us—
> Daunting us—Onward!   Graves under us silent.
>
>   —GOETHE.

> ' We see the end—but not the path.
> O'er mountain tops with fainting hearts and weary,
>   We yet must climb;
> Then in the valleys, desolate and dreary,
>   Abide our time.'

(3)

' The undeveloped flower-cup
            Will persevere,
And rear its scented chalice up,
Enbalming all its heart cells through
With sweetness.—Another year.'

For I the Lord thy God will hold thy right hand,
saying unto thee, Fear not, I will help thee.—And
she called the name of the Lord that spake unto her,
Thou God seest me.

2. To stretch toward the Infinite is the first effort.
The second, is to connect the Infinite with our personal sphere, our movements, interests, and destinies.
The mind of man, gazing up to the Infinite Nature
with mingled reverence and trust, opens and utters
itself to Omniscience. His awful presence is un-
utterably near to us. The open Infinite Eye gazes
upon us every moment. When this faith is once
reached, life becomes invested with wondrous sanc-
tity.—YOUNG.

All complete knowledge involves the taking of
manifold elements, separating and sorting them, and
finally comprehending them in Unity. So the individual finite reason, if at all, must know the universal reason; and the finite may so know the universal
as to see in it that the universal must be personal.—
HICKOK.

3. *If I take the wings of the morning and dwell*
in the uttermost parts of the sea: even there shall thy
hand lead me, and thy right hand shall hold me.

If we consider him in his omnipresence; his being passes through, actuates, and supports the whole frame of nature. His creation and every part of it is full of him. There is nothing he has made, that is either so distant, so little, or so inconsiderable, which he does not essentially inhabit. His substance is within the substance of every being, whether material or immaterial, and as intimately present to it, as that being is to itself. It would be an imperfection in him, were he able to remove out of one place into another, or to withdraw himself from anything he has created, or from any part of that space which is so diffused and spread abroad to infinity. In short, to speak of him in the language of an old philosopher:—He is a being whose centre is everywhere, and his circumference nowhere.—SPECTATOR.

We must believe him great without quantity, omnipresent without place, everlasting without time, and containing all things without extent; and when our thoughts are come to the highest, let us stop, wonder, and adore!—HALL.

For thus saith the high and lofty One that inhabiteth eternity, whose name is Holy, I dwell in the high and holy place, with him also that is of a contrite and humble spirit.

* I have felt
A presence that disturbs me with the joy
Of elevated thoughts; a sense sublime,
Of something far more deeply interfused—
Well pleased to recognize

In nature and the language of the sense,
The anchor of my purest thoughts, the nurse,
The guide, the guardian of my heart, and soul
Of all my moral being.—WORDSWORTH.

I meditate on thee in the night watches.

'In the still silence of the voiceless night,
  When, chased by airy dreams, the slumbers flee,
  Whom in the darkness doth my spirit seek,
          O God, but thee?

' And if there be a weight upon my breast,
  Some vague impression of the day foregone,
  Scarce knowing what it is, I fly to thee
          And lay it down.

' Or if it be the heaviness that comes
  In token of anticipated ill,
  My bosom takes no heed of what it is,
          Since 'tis thy will.

' More tranquil than the stillness of the night,
  More peaceful than the silence of that hour,
  More blest than anything, my spirit lies
          Beneath thy power.'

4. At a certain time in the course of my inward
personal history, I found myself in a state of inward
desolation. God seemed to be hidden from my view;
Christ as a distinct object of conception was withdrawn. I found nothing of that familiar and delightful access to the great Source of life, whether
denominated God or Christ, to which I had been accustomed. The beautiful ministry of angelic and
spiritual experiences had departed. And, in addi-

tion to this, there was a weakening and disruption of the ties which bound me to many of my earthly friends. Both inwardly and outwardly was one of vacuity and deprivation which apparently wanted nothing to its completeness. It reminded me of what I had once known in the deserts of Sinai, where standing on the tops of the highest mountains, I beheld around me nothing but the rugged cliffs.

Finding myself in this arid and painful condition of things, which, perhaps for the sake of convenience may be denominated in the language of the old mystics, the 'spiritual wilderness,' I remained for a time in a sort of amazement, unable to understand its nature, or its meaning. At last aroused from the inactivity and confusion of spirit which naturally attended it, I ventured in my supplications to ask the Lord what was the cause of these unlooked-for experiences, and what instruction he wished me to derive from them ? For I knew, though he was hidden in great and unprecedented mystery, He must be somewhere, where He could listen to the sound of my voice. For a time no responsive utterance came, neither to the outward ear where I did not look for it; nor to the interior of the soul where I had often heard it in suggestions and intimations which left no doubt of the divinity of their origin. After such a time as seemed necessary to impress me fully with the fact of this great desolation, and also train my heart to the unwavering acceptance of it as a condi-

tion of things which had its significancy and its results, and to dwell quietly amid its clouds and darkness, I received from time to time, and through
those interior sources which the Holy Spirit knows
how to open and employ, such intimations and teachings as became afterwards of great value. With a
heart devoted to God no longer seek him in the
heavens above, or the earth beneath, nor in any
locality which will have the effect to limit his existence, but recognize Him as the great fact of the universe, separate from no place or part, but revealed
in all places, and in all things and events, moment
by moment. . . It is moreover, one of those things
which in any true philosophy of the universe will be
found to lie at the foundation of the greatest problem
of what constitutes the highest amount of human
happiness. Meeting God in the present moment we
shall meet Him always the same but always new:
always unchanged in his essence, but changing always in his incidents. The divine moment, lifting
as it emerges into being, the veil that rests upon
forms and places, and actions and events, opens that
little eyelid of eternity and reveals God; not in a
perpetual identity of manifestation which would tire
our perception and annul our growth, but in all possible varieties. He stands before us sometimes in the
storm, and sometimes in the sunshine; sometimes
in the waste howling wilderness, and sometimes in
the field of flowers; in the palace and the prison, in

friendship and enmity, in joy and sorrow. And thus He is always revealing, step by step, in harmony with the nature and extent of our own capacity the infinitudes of existence; and always affording new elements of knowledge, new tests of strength, and new foundations and appliances of growth and happiness. Those who live in the divine moment are relieved in a great degree from the perplexities of conjectures and calculations, and cannot be said in the usual sense of the terms to have any plans of action. Being in harmony with the facts of the present moment, it is the law of their condition, that they shall do the work which it is given them to do,—so that it can justly be said, that the mind of the Infinite is substituted for his own, and that God plans for him. And hence it is, that the one great sign of the practical recognition of the divine moment is constant calmness and peace of mind. Events and things come with the moment, but God with them too, written all over with the divinity of wisdom and the glory of the promises.—UPHAM.

5. The person who has a firm trust in the Supreme Being is powerful in his power, wise by his wisdom, happy by his happiness. He reaps the benefit of every divine attribute, and loses his own insufficiency in the fullness of infinite perfection. To make our lives more easy to us, we are commanded to put our trust in him, who is thus able to relieve and succor us; the divine goodness having

made such a reliance a duty, notwithstanding we should have been miserable had it been forbidden us.—ADDISON.

Jonah cried: *They that observe lying vanities forsake their own mercy.*

I will that men pray everywhere, lifting up holy hands without wrath or doubting.

> Why wilt thou now give place to fear?
> How cans't thou want if he provide?
> Or lose thy way with such a guide?
> Slowly, alas! the mind receives
> The comfort that our Maker gives.

' When trial comes, all the consolation that abounds with it, is the result of a practiced faith.'

6. In two several ways I am wont to visit mine elect, namely with temptation and consolation. And I daily read two lessons to them; one in reproving their vices; another in exhorting them to the increase of their virtues.—KEMPIS.

> Not in one golden year
> Shall thy soul ripen to its glorious prime,
> And the rich fruitage mark the harvest time:
> But slowly, day by day,
> In the full sunshine and the midnight gloom,
> Shall grow the fruit that crowns its wondrous bloom.
> —EMILY MILLER.

The blade—the ear—the full corn in the ear.

Nature rightly understood is a slow worker. Not suddenly, not by a single stroke does she accomplish her changes. Little by little is her rule, and patiently, watchfully she awaits the result.—L. A. O.

For so the Lord said unto me, I will take my rest, and I will consider in my dwelling place, like a clear heat upon herbs, like a cloud of dew in the heat of harvest.

It intimates that the great God has a perfect undisturbed enjoyment of himself in the midst of all the tosses and changes of this world; sits even upon the floods undisturbed. The Eternal Mind is always easy. He will consider over it what is best to be done, and will be sure to do all for the best.—HENRY.

' The Great Soul that sits on the throne of the universe is not, never was, and never will be in a hurry. In the realm of nature everything has been wrought out in the august consciousness of infinite leisure. There is no well-doing, no godlike doing, that is not patient doing. There is no great achievement that is not the result of patient working and waiting. There is no royal road to anything. One thing at a time, all things in succession. That which grows fast withers as rapidly. That which grows slowly, slowly endures. Think how patiently he bears with your impatience. Listen! there comes no outcry from the heavens to still all this wild unrest, but gently, patiently, the ministry of nature and Providence proceeds from day to day.'

This mixed divine and human weaving we call Life:—wherein the fabric seems so often, faulty, where much seems lost, left out, or wrongly joined, where correspondence is delayed, and full-matched beauty missed; where colors are confused, where the pattern being vast may never quite unroll to earthly vision; where Patience keeps her foot upon the treadle and Faith must stand with fervent eyes beside the springing shuttle.—MRS. WHITNEY.

Be not sudden, take God's work together, and do not judge of it by parcels or pieces. It is indeed all wisdom and righteousness; but we shall best discern the beauty of it, when we look on it in the frame, and when it shall be fully completed and finished, and our eyes enlightened to take a fuller and completer view of it than we can have here.—LEIGHTON.

> In the woeful waste of famine,
> And the scourge of pestilence;
> In all woes and wrongs around us,
> •In all strife of man with man;
> In all discords that confound us,
> Runs his great harmonious plan.—BURLEIGH.

7. *What profit shall we have if we pray unto Him?*

> 'Prayer makes the darkened cloud withdraw,
> Brings every blessing from above.
> Restraining prayer—we cease to fight.'

'Telegraphic communication with heaven closed.' All our hopes lie in this higher sphere of thought

and emotion. To this region, the only key is prayer.
—PHELPS.

Speak Lord, for thy servant heareth. In thy faithfulness answer me and in thy righteousness.

Make me sensible of real answers to actual requests, as evidences of an interchange between myself on earth and my Saviour in heaven.—CHALMERS.

'A goodly man, the master of an American ship, during one of his voyages, found his ship surrounded by fog for days, and became very anxious respecting her safety. He went down to the cabin and prayed. The thought struck him, if he had with confidence committed his soul to God, he might certainly commit his ship to him ; and so accordingly he gave all into the hands of God, and felt at perfect peace ; but still he prayed that if he would be pleased to give a cloudless sky at twelve o'clock, he should like to take an observation, to ascertain their real position, and whether they were on the right course. He came on deck with the quadrant under his coat. As it was thick and drizzling, the men looked at him with amazement. He went down again to his cabin, prayed and came up. There still seemed no hope. Again he went down and prayed, and again he appeared on deck with his quadrant in his hand. It was now ten minutes to twelve o'clock, and still there was no appearance of a change ; but he stood on deck waiting on the Lord, when, in a few minutes, the mist seemed folded up and rolled away by an

omnipotent and invisible hand ; the sun shone clearly
from the blue vault of heaven, and there stood the
man of prayer, with the quadrant in his hand ; but
so awe-struck did he feel, and so ' dreadful ' was that
place, that he could scarcely take advantage of the
answer of his prayer. He however succeeded,
though with trembling hands, and found to his comfort that all was well.   But no sooner had he finished
taking his observation than the mist rolled back over
the heavens.'

I have sometimes tried to conceive a panorama of
the history of one prayer. I have endeavored to
follow it from its inception in a human mind through
its utterance by human lips, and in its flight up to
the ear of Him who is its Hearer because He has
been also its Inspirer, and on its journey around to
the unnumbered points in the organism of His
decrees which this feeble human voice reaches, and
from which it entices a responsive vibration, because
this is also a decree of as venerable antiquity as
theirs : and in its return from those altitudes with
its golden train of blessings to which eternal counsels have paid tribute at His bidding. I have
endeavored to form some conception thus of the
methods by which this omnipotence of poor human
speech gains its end without a shock to the system
of the universe, with not so much as a whit of
change to a course of a leaf falling in the air. A
holy prayer is the spirit of God speaking through

the infirmities of the human soul; God's breath in man returning to his birth. We scarcely utter hyperbole in saying, that prayer is the Divine Mind communing with itself through finite wants, through the woes of helplessness, through the clinging instincts of weakness. On this side the judgment, no other conception of the presence of God is so profound as that which is realized in our souls every time we offer a genuine prayer. God is not only with us but within us.—PHELPS.

Moses wist not that the skin of his face shone while he talked with them.

' Much communion with God will communicate a glory to his character which the good man himself will be the last to discover. The man who has walked in the garden of the Lord can not keep the secret. His very raiment exhales spice and odor ! '

> When one that holds communion with the skies,
> Has filled his urn where those pure waters rise,
> And once more mingles with us meaner things,
> 'Tis e'en as if an angel shook his wings.
> Immortal fragrance fills the circuit wide,
> That tells us when his treasures are supplied.

—COWPER.

8. *I am the Almighty God, walk before me, and be thou perfect.*

Delight thyself also in the Lord, and he shall give thee the desires of thine heart.

God's providences depend upon men's interpretations. When what a man wants is put within his reach he always thinks it is a providence. That part of you that hears God speaking determines what it is that He says. The only time that it is safe to give a man the desires of his heart is when his heart is fixed on God. It is conceded by all that if a man seeks his own highest culture and makes manhood the real aim of his being, it is true that by seeking God and His righteousness first, he shall best attain to the desires of his life.

—BEECHER.

No man knows what divine power or what divine peace is, until he is in sympathy with God, so that he can feel that all things are his because all things are renounced by him.—ROBERTSON.

9. *Whereby shall I know that I shall inherit it? Behold a smoking furnace and a burning lamp.*

The holy men of old who had revelations from God, had outward signs besides the internal light of assurance in their own minds to testify to them that it was from God. Where the truth embraced is consonant to the revelation in the written word of God, or the action conformable to the dictates of right reason or holy writ, we may be assured that we run no risk in entertaining it as such. But it is not the strength of our private persuasion within ourselves that can warrant it to be a light or notion from heaven.

How distinguish between delusions and the inspirations of the Holy Ghost. Satan can transform himself into an angel of light.

There is no error to be named which has not had its professors: and a man shall never want crooked paths to walk in if he thinks that he is in the right way whenever he has the footsteps of others to follow.—LOCKE.

We are not warranted under the Christian dispensation to require any miraculous intimation of the Divine Will: for the word of God alone is our guide and warrant.

Remember thy word unto thy servant upon which thou hast caused me to hope.

' Remember, O Lord, that Thou hast given this promise and encouraged my hope in it: and whatever appearances may be, I must wait and pray for the accomplishment of it, for Thou wilt never disappoint the expectation which Thy own word hath excited.'

' Without Thy counsel and providence, and without cause nothing cometh to pass in the earth.'

10. *I wait for the Lord, my soul doth wait, and in His word do I hope.*

' A strange sweet sorrow about this deep trust— a repose born of sorrow and pain. I never felt it in a joyful mood: happiness never goes down so deep into the soul or raises the spirit up into such a calm solemn nearness to the eternal.'

Blessed are all they that wait for Him.

'Little can we by the beginning of any action or
event guess at God's intention in the conclusion.
God sometimes disappoints us, exceeding our
expectations, as well as at others falling short of
them. Saul went to seek his father's asses, but
found a kingdom and a crown.'

It is doing a right thing and waiting to-day and
weeks and months for a reward: so long that when
it comes you cannot identify it with the action performed. It is living and working for truth and
righteousness, and let the results come and mingle
with the course of affairs. It is having faith in
rectitude and in God, though you do not have visible
results on which to base that faith. It is this that
is the difficult thing. Here is the ground of super-
lative training. God knows that you are going to
live after to-day and to-morrow. He sees a road
of exaltation in which you are to walk. He remem-
bers that he is to lift you up and crown you with
eternal honors in heaven.—BEECHER.

'If need be, one must learn to wait his whole
life, and expect the time of opportunity in another
world. Crimes of every character, diseases of every
name, infamy and shame, are the fit ills of him who
will not learn to wait.'

'Patience, what is long sought comes when
unsought.'

*And blessed is she that believed, for there shall be
a performance of those things which were told her
from the Lord.*

'All they that make his laws their choice shall
in his promises rejoice.'

*For he performeth the thing that is appointed for
me.*

11. *According to your faith be it unto you.*

He follows the Ruler with a full knowledge of
the case, with warmest sympathy, but no flush of
haste is on his cheek, nor does a line of impatience
ruffle his placid brow. He will satisfy the Ruler's
longing, but not till he has taught him a high lesson
of patience and faith. . . 'She is dead, trouble
not the master.' Faith reels under the blow. But
Jesus will not permit it to fail. Everything depends
on that mustard seed of faith in the Ruler's soul.
Such is the decree of heaven—why, we need not ask
too curiously,—that faith must wait for the gifts of
grace. Faith must pluck the ripened fruit which
can fall only into the believer's hand. Through all
the previous suspense and tension of faith in the
Ruler's soul, Christ has been preparing him to
receive the answer of his prayer. This preparation
was painful indeed. It consisted in taking down
the supports of nature, that the sustaining power of
grace might have room. While he rested in his
own methods, fixed his own limits of time, and shut
up the Holy One within the barrier of his own short
sightedness, faith was but feebly at work. He had
no adequate perception of the power he addressed.
We know not what our faith may cost: but if we

will boldly ask, if we have faith to hope, and patience to wait we shall, like the Ruler, rejoice at last in the power and grace of Jesus Christ.

—BEECHER.

Trust and distrust are the day and night of the human soul. Out of the one issue light and courage, life and strength, liberty and joy: out of the other darkness and apprehension, weakness, bondage, and unhappiness. When Jesus said, According to your faith be it unto you, He uttered an infinite truth, that like the century plant presents its mysterious and patient leaves to the gaze of successive generations, and only opens its wondrous blossoms to later eyes.—HELMER.

It is impossible to calculate the effects which may be produced by distrust and suspense. They make the heart collapse, and wither the character. I believe that universal distrust would ruin any character.—ROBERTSON.

> Mistrust of good success hath done this deed.
> O hateful error, melancholy's child!
> Why dost thou show to the apt thoughts of men
> The things that are not?
> Alas! thou hast misconstrued everything,
> Didst thou not hear their shouts?
>
> —JULIUS CÆSAR.

The steward of my house is this Eliezur of Damascus.

'He must yet live upon assurances and promises

withoct any earthly prospect. This works within
him in a way of secret anguish.'

Let us trust the time will come when the present
moment shall be no longer irksome; when we shall
not borrow all our happiness from hope which is at
last to end in disappointment.—JOHNSON.

*O Lord, thou hast deceived me and I was deceived:
thou art stronger than I and hast prevailed.*

'In a strict sense the Supreme Being can neither
change His mind, nor falsify His word; but He can
make those changes in the course of His providence
that have that appearance.' 'God may command
what He has not decreed, as in slaying Isaac; and
decrees what He does not command, as in the death
of His Son. Essential to prove the moral character
and afford an opportunity for man to show his allegi-
ance to God.'

'Truth is truth to the end of the reckoning.'

*Establish thy word to thy servant who is devoted to
thy fear.*

> Is not thy grace as mighty now
> As when Elijah felt its power?—
> When glory beamed from Moses' brow,
> Or Job endured the trying hour?

*O arm of the Lord; awake, as in the ancient days,
in the generations of old.*

> Has not the Lord denied his aid
> When earth and hell against me rose?
> It is not so, but so it looks,

And we lose courage then,
And doubts will come if God hath kept
His promises to men.

Shall not the Judge of all the earth do right?

God's justice is a bed,
Where we our weary heads may lay,
And weary with ourselves may sleep
Our discontent away.

'The language of some implies that the God of the universe had let go the helm· or ceased to rule righteously. .

'The enemy is sometimes gratified by an arrangement of outward dispensations exactly suited to favor his assaults; so that the believer's path seems wholly obstructed. The Lord himself appears to forsake him, or even to fight against him, and his appointments are thought contrary to his promises. This gives Satan an opportunity of suggesting hard thoughts of God and his ways; doubts about the truths of the Scriptures, and desponding fears of a fatal event. Many such fiery darts may be repelled or quenched by the shield of faith; but there are seasons when they are poured in so incessantly, and receive such plausibility from facts, that the enemy wounds him in his faith, understanding and conversation.

'Bitter anguish have I borne,
Keen regret my heart hath torn,
Satan blinded me with lies'—

He hath also taken me by my neck and shaken me to pieces, and set me up for his mark. Not for any injustice in mine hands.

I have learned also to dread thy unsearchable judgments, who afflictest the just with the wicked, though not without equity and justice.—KEMPIS.

'The Lord in His favor hath fixed the believer's safety firm as the deep-rooted mountains: but in everything else he may expect to be shaken.'

'Life has such hard conditions, that every dear and precious gift, every rare virtue, every pleasant faculty, every genial endowment, love, hope, joy, wit, sprightliness, must sometimes be cast into the crucible to distill the one elixir—patience.'

13. *He hath made me desolate and faint all the day.*

'With weary steps I loiter on,
   Though always under altered skies,
   The purple from the distance dies,
My prospect and horizon gone.
   'When the star of the evening shines out,
      Large and fair in the west,
   You will gather no hope from its rays,
      No promise of rest.'

Remove thy stroke away from me. I am consumed by the blow of thine hand.

At that time I was suffering under one of those heaven-sent blows, under which the strongest and most philosophic succumb for a time—many forever. As I was neither strong nor philosophic, the greatest

affliction man can suffer passed over me, and left me
walking, eating, sleeping, but in the manner of those
animals to which we anatomists attribute little or no
self-consciousness in their actions, and no pleasure
in the fulfilment of them. We may be wrong ; the
hungry looking arms of the anemone may obey a
more than mere unconscious stimulus when they
touch and secure their prey, but at all events, man
who possesses all the nervous organization for being,
doing and suffering is in as doubtful a case when in
such circumstances as those to which I allude.—
HARPER'S WEEKLY.

15. *The heart knoweth his own bitterness.*

Deep down within the labyrinth of the breast,
  Close veiled in shadows black as midnight air,
A temple stands ; by human art ne'er dressed,
  For God's own mighty hand has reared it there.

An altar high those temple walls contain,
  On which life's sacrifices oft are made ;
Its surface streaked with many a bloody stain,
  That marked the cruel, sacrificial blade
Within that gloomy, shadow-drap'd abode,
  The *inmost soul* unseen and unknown dwells,
And bears about in solitude its load
  Of secret joys and griefs it never tells.—G. W. S.

Who does not know that all the sternest conflicts
of life can never be recorded ? Every human soul
must walk alone through the darkest and most dan-
gerous paths of its spiritual pilgrimage ; absolutely

alone with God! Much from which we suffer most acutely could never be revealed to others; still more, could never be understood if it were revealed; and still more, ought never to be repeated if it could be understood.—Mrs. Child.

16. *They shall put you out of the synagogues.*

What is a little scourge of the tongue? What is a thrusting out of the synagogue? The time of temptation will be when we are thrust into an inner prison and feel the iron entering into our souls. God's people may be permitted to forsake us for a while, but the Lord Jesus can stand by us. And if thou, O dearest Redeemer, wilt strengthen me in my inner man, let enemies plunge me into a fiery furnace, or throw me into a den of lions! Let us suffer for Jesus with a cheerful heart. His love will sweeten every cup though never so bitter.—White-field.

17. *I will show him how great things he must suffer for my name.*

'A steady, wise design through all their sufferings.'

In this life sorrows are crowned kings. Their crowns are iron. Midnight is in their eye. Awful sternness seems to be in their hearts. Men lie as victims in dungeons under the dominion of sorrow, and know not that in this strange way, God prepares men for coronation, and that these stern-browed kings of misery are after all but angels of mercy and of love.—Beecher.

Christian life is not visible success; very often the apparent opposite of success. It is·the resurrection of Christ working itself out in us; but it very often is the cross of Christ imprinting itself on us very sharply. The highest prize God has to give us here is martyrdom. The highest style of life is heroic, enduring, manly love. The noblest coronet any son of man can wear, is a crown of thorns.—ROBERTSON.

> * 'the chastening rod
> Grows cool beneath his blessed feet,
> Whose form is as the son of God.'

18. *But he knoweth the way that I take; when* **he** *hath tried me I shall come forth as gold.*

> Rejoice, our Marah's bitter springs
> Are sweetened; on our ground of grief
> Rise day by day, in strong relief,
> The prophecies of better things.—WHITTIER.

May we be divinely strengthened to bear, and made wise to improve whatever dispensation is in store for us; may we be enlightened to see in whatever good or ill fortune shall ensue, the loving kindness of a Father whose very chastenings are more beneficent than the fullest gratification of our desires.—GREELEY.

Satan hath·desired to have you that he may sift you as wheat. But I have prayed for thee that thy faith fail not: and when thou art converted, strengthen thy brethren.

Be thou of such good courage, and so patient in hope, that when inward comfort is withdrawn, thou mayest prepare thy heart to suffer greater things, and do not justify thyself as though thou oughtest not to suffer these afflictions, or any so great; but justify me in whatsoever I appoint, and still praise my holy name. Stand to my good-will and thou shalt suffer no detriment at all.—KEMPIS.

Faith loves to let him have his own way—extracts the honey of joy out of every daisy by the wayside—presses the wine of contentment out of every cluster of God's promises.—BEECHER.

> ' With cheerful feet the path of duty run,
> God nothing does nor sufters to be done,
> But what thou would'st thyself, could'st thou but see
> Through all events of things as well as he.'

19. *All her persecutors overtook her in the midst of the straits.*

Frail and changeable in virtue, you might perhaps have been good under a series of auspicious circum- stances, but the glory had been to be victoriously good against malignant ones.—-FOSTER.

> * * thou shalt know ere long,
> Know how sublime a thing it is
> To suffer and be strong.

LONGFELLOW.

Because thou shalt forget thy misery and remember it as waters that pass away. For he shall not much remember the days of his life because God answereth him in the joy of his heart.

> 'I look to find thee in thy word
> Or at thy table meet.'
> I wait till from my veiled brows shall fall
> This baffling cloud, this wearying thrall
> Which holds me now from knowing all.

—M. C. A.

> 'Hid in the everlasting deeps,
> The silent God His secret keeps.'

If this invisible Being would only break that mysterious silence in which he has wrapt himself, we feel that a single word from his mouth would be worth a world of darkling speculations.

—CHALMERS.

'In the great mirror of eternity all the events of this checkered scene will be reflected. Pry not, then, curiously; pronounce not censoriously on God's dealings with thee. Wait with patience till the grand day of disclosures.'

In the latter days ye shall consider it perfectly.

'But in this life though there might be growth, it was the growth that comes from the pain endured with patience, through self-control maintained in the suspense and the anguish of death!

> 'In thee I trust, to thee sign,
> And lift my heavy soul on high;
> For thee sit waiting all the day,
> And wear the tiresome hours away.'

What does anxiety about future contingencies bring thee .but sorrow upon sorrow, and consuming cares and disappointments,—anxieties from various attrition? This mental condition robs life of its honey.—BEECHER.

Instead of learning the designs and character of the Almighty from his own mouth, we sit in judg ment on them, and make our conjecture of what they should be, take the precedency of his revelation of what they are. We do him the same injustice that we do to an acquaintance whose proceedings and intentions we venture to pronounce upon, while we refuse him a hearing, or turn away from the letter in which he explains himself.—CHALMERS.

Wherefore hath the Lord pronounced all this great evil against us ?

He thwarts you in the gaining of some object; hard, but good. He is far better to you than if he had helped you to it..—SHEPARD.

I am the Lord thy God which teacheth thee to profit, which leadeth thee by the way that thou shouldest go. I have called him; I have brought him and he shall make his way prosperous.

' Brought him step by step, quite beyond his own intentions.'

20. *I will allure her and bring her into the wilder-ness and give her her vineyards from thence.*

The promises designed to allure till their higher signification is reached.

The letter is but the body of the spirit in which it dwells, or the scaffolding which surrounds the building while the walls are going up, or the form which the living substance puts on to manifest itself and to perform its functions.—D. L. L.

And this is what God does. His promises are true, though illusive; truer than we at first take them to be. We work for a mean, low, sensual happiness, all the while he is leading us on to a spiritual blessedness unfathomably deep. This is the life of faith. We do not preach that all is disappointment, the dreary creed of sentimentalism: but we preach that nothing here is disappointment, if rightly understood. He in whom God-like character dwells, has all the universe for his own.

—ROBERTSON.

Behold the days come that I will perform that good thing I have promised.

22.   In thine own dull and dreary state,
To work and patiently to wait.
Little thou think'st in thy despair,
How soon the o'ershadowed sun may shine,
And e'en the dulling clouds combine
To bless with lights and hues divine,
    That region dark and bare—
Those sad and sinful thoughts of thine.

They that are Christ's have crucified the flesh with the affections and lusts.

If thou wouldst be faithful to do the work that God hath appointed thee to do in this world for His

name, then beware thou do not stop and stick when
hard work comes before thee. The word and spirit
of God come sometimes like chain-shot to us, as if
they would cut down all—as when Abraham was
to offer up Isaac. Oh how willingly would our flesh
and blood escape the cross for Christ! With
Ephraim, we like to tread out the corn, and to hear
those pleasant songs and music that gospel sermons
make, where only grace is preached, and nothing of
our own duty as to works of self-denial.—BUNYAN.

23. *Lord, I will follow Thee, but let me go bid
farewell.—If any man come to me and hate not his
father and mother and wife and children, and brethren
and sisters, yea, and his own life also, he cannot be
my disciple.*

O merciful Jesus, grant me but a small portion of
Thy hearty affectionate love, that my faith may
become more strong. How can I bear up myself
in this miserable life, unless Thou strengthen me
with Thy mercy and grace?—KEMPIS.

*As for me is my complaint to man, and if it were
so why should not my spirit be troubled?*

*Lord, all my desire is before Thee. And the Lord
said unto me, Let it suffice thee, speak no more unto
me of this matter.*

That prayer which does not succeed in moderating
our wish, in changing the passionate desire into
still submission; the anxious, tumultuous expecta-

tion into silent surrender, is no true prayer, and
proves that we have not the spirit of prayer.

—PHELPS.

24.   'Thankful I take the cup from Thee,
            Prepared and mingled by Thy skill,
          Though bitter to the taste it be.'

Blessed and true is the comfort which is received
inwardly from the truth.   Let this be my consolation, to be cheerfully willing to do without all
human comfort.—KEMPIS.

When our energies demand sustenance they cannot get, when our will strains after a path it may
not follow, we need neither starve from inanition,
nor stand still in despair.   We have but to seek
another nourishment for the mind, as strong as the
forbidden food it longed to taste, and perhaps purer,
and to hew out for the adventurous foot a road as
direct and broad as the one fortune has blocked up
against us, if rougher than it.—CHARLOTTE BRONTE.

We talked about the different courses through
which life ran.   She (Miss Bronte) said in her own
composed manner, as if she had accepted the theory
as a fact, that she believed some were appointed
beforehand to sorrow and much disappointment.
That it did not fall to the lot of all, as Scripture
told us, to have their lines fall in pleasant places:
that it was well for those who had rougher paths to
perceive that such was God's will concerning them,

and try to moderate their expectations, leaving hope to those of a different doom, and seeking patience and resignation as the virtues they were to cultivate. She was trying to school herself against ever anticipating any pleasure: that it was better to be brave and submit faithfully: there was some good reason which we should know in time why sorrow and disappointment were to be the lot of some on earth. It was better to acknowledge this, and face out the truth in a religious life.—Mrs. GASKELL.

Every passion not merely kept in abeyance by asceticism, but subdued by a higher impulse, is so much character strengthened—BEECHER.

' Self-indulgence has turned our love into selfishness, and now we shall return to love only through self-denial.'

You would make a law for God prescribing the kind of death by which he shall destroy your self-love, and then, too, on the condition that self-love shall not die.—FENELON.

Give up anything, bear anything; do anything, wait and suffer, work and pray. This is to be my heaven to see Him who fainted under the cross for me.—KEMPIS.

25. *I stand and knock.* What then is this knocking? It consists of every influence that addresses man's nobler nature and tends to bring him into right relations to God.—BEECHER

*2

Come in, come in, thou waiting One,
Thou man of kingly mien !
I open now this door of stone :
How patient thou hast been !

ı heard thee knocking long ago,
But there were guests within.
To turn them out I was too slow,
I loved each bosom sin.

But now come in ! the table spread !
Come in, I'll sup with thee ;
Pour out the wine ıhy soul hath bled,
And break the bread for me.

I charge you, tempters, never more
Invade this sacred place ;
Since Jesus has passed through the door,
And I have seen his face.

Joy makes me humbler than my sin,
That I should see his glory !
That I should say Christ enter in,
And know thee, and adore thee !

As my Father loved me so I also love you, said I
unto my beloved disciples, whom certainly I sent not
out to temporal joys, but to great conflicts ; not to
honors, but to contempts ; not to idleness, but to
labors ; not to rest, but to bring forth much fruit with
patience. Go forward—the crown is before thee—a
short labor and a great reward.—KEMPIS.

When the will of God is known, wish it not
changed. Cherish no wish to do otherwise than as

God allows. We must not only acknowledge, but acquiesce in the hand of God appointing us our lot.— HENRY.

26. *He shall choose our inheritance for us.*

'He sets us in our appointed place; gives us His Holy Spirit, His word, the examples of His saints, bright promises, awful warnings; and then He expects us to do our part earnestly and seriously, without wavering or trifling.'

Working in you that which is well-pleasing in His sight.

'He leaves His servants each to work out some side of Christian truth, dividing to every man severally as He will, according to the power of each mind and the needs of each situation.'

'How slow we are to learn this simple truth, that we are safer and happier just where God would have us be, and doing just what He would have us do.'

Blessed art thou—for flesh and blood hath not revealed it unto thee.—See that ye refuse not Him that speaketh.—And look that thou make them after the pattern that was showed thee in the mount.

Sir Isaac Newton completed in his own person the character of the true philosopher. He not only saw the general principle, but he obeyed it. He both betook himself to the drudgery of observation, and he endured the pain which every mind must suffer in the act of renouncing its old habits of conception. Have manhood and philosophy enough to make a similar sacrifice. It is not enough that the Bible be acknowledged as the only authentic source of information respecting the details of that moral economy which the Supreme Being has instituted for the government of the intelligent beings who occupy this globe.—CHALMERS.

What portion then, of so high and sacred a mystery shall an unworthy sinner, dust and ashes, be able to search out and comprehend? It is thy work and no human power.—KEMPIS.

Do ye not understand, neither remember the five loaves of the five thousand, and how many baskets ye took up?

Deal courageously and the Lord will be with you.

There is a real appearance of somewhat of great weight in this matter, though he is not able to satisfy himself thoroughly about it. Evidence which keeps the mind in doubt.—BUTLER.

If this counsel or this work be of men, it will come to nought. But if it be of God ye cannot overthrow it.

'Time overthrows the illusions of opinion, but establishes the decisions of nature.'

'So far as a man is true to virtue, to veracity and justice, to equity and charity and the right of the case in whatever he is concerned, so far, he is on the side of the divine administration and co-operates with it.'

27. Henceforth to holier purposes I devote myself.—F. F.

I prepare myself with cheerful willingness to be despised and forsaken of all creatures, and to be esteemed quite entirely nothing. I cannot obtain inward peace and stability, nor be spiritually enlightened, nor be fully united unto thee.—KEMPIS.

> 'Dark, till in me thine image shine,
> And lost I am till thou art mine.'

If thine eye offend thee pluck it out.
Through desire a man having separated himself seeketh and intermeddleth with all wisdom.

> * separate from the world,
> His breast might duly take and strongly keep
> The print of heaven.'

> 'From nature's every path retreat.'

And the Lord shut him in.
Draw nigh to the Lord and he will draw nigh to you.

If too, thou stand steadfast in all circumstances and do not weigh the things which thou seest and hearest by the outward appearance nor with a carnal eye, but presently in every affair dost enter with Moses into the tabernacle to ask counsel of the Lord, thou shalt sometimes near the Divine Oracle, and shalt return instructed concerning many things, both present and to come.—KEMPIS.

Samuel could distinguish between the impulse,

quite a human one, which would have made him select
Eliab out of Jesse's sons, and the deeper judgment
by which the Lord said, Look not on his countenance
or on the height of his stature; because I have refused him; for the Lord seeth not as man seeth; for
man looketh on the outward appearance, but the
Lord looketh on the heart. Deep truth of character
is required; the whispering voices get mixed together; we dare not abide by our own thoughts.
Only given to the habitually true to know the difference. God is near you. Throw yourself fearlessly
upon him, trembling mortal! There is an unknown
might within your soul which will wake when you
command it.—ROBERTSON.

'Energies that long have slumbered
  In its trackless depths unnumbered;
  Speak the word; the power divinest
  Will awake, if thou inclinest.'

*Hearken, O daughter, and consider and incline thine
ear, forget also thine own people and thy father's
house, so shall the king greatly desire thy beauty, for
he is thy Lord and worship thou Him.*

Whoso withdraweth himself from his acquaintance
and friends, God will draw near to him with His
holy angels.

Withdraw thyself from gadding idly, and speaking
vainly.—KEMPIS.

'A wise and pious man before all other knowledge
prefers that of God and his own soul.'

'He who does not know himself cannot know others. If you analyze one drop of water from a spring you know what every drop contains. If you know one man—yourself, you know them all in outline and in elementary principles. Learning your own heart, you learn the hearts of others; studying the secret springs and motives and impulses that govern you, and making due allowance for the peculiarities of constitution and training and surroundings, you may draw very good conclusions concerning the characters of those around you and the considerations which will naturally impress their minds.'

'We know that these were felt by him,
- For these are felt by all.'

29. *Blessed is the man whom thou choosest and causest to approach unto thee.*

'My soul invited by thy word stands watching at thy gate.' Since therefore it is thy pleasure and thou hast commanded that it should be so, this thy condescension is also dearly pleasing unto me, and O, that my iniquity may be no hindrance.—KEMPIS.

30. *Cease ye from man whose breath is in his nostrils · for wherein is he to be accounted of? I will counsel thee, mine eye shall be upon thee. And thine ears shall hear a word behind thee saying, This is the way, walk ye in it.*

'An incomparable distance between the things which the imperfect imagine in their conceits and those which the illuminated are enabled to behold through revelation from above.'

'The former stagger in their counsels, are unstable and unsteady, and stumble at everything that lies in their way.'

Enoch walked with God.

Powerfully holding thee up, lest by thine own weight thou fall down to the things of earth.

Lord, I stand in need of much greater grace, if I ought to reach that pitch where neither man nor any creature shall be a hindrance unto me.

A man ought therefore to mount over all creatures, and perfectly to go out of himself and stand in ecstasy of mind and see that Thou, the Creator of all things, hast nothing amongst creatures like unto Thyself.—KEMPIS.

But the soul that ascends to the worship of the great God is plain and true: has no rose color, no fine friends, no chivalry, no adventures: does not want admiration, dwells in the hour that now is; in the earnest experience of the common day, by reason of the present moment and the mere trifle, having become porous to thought and bibulous of the sea of light.—EMERSON.

Surely the Lord is in this place, and I knew it not.

'So might we house a gentle guest,
The Comforter in our lone breast,
And feel e'en here the perfect rest

Which follows when our will is past
Into our Father's will at last—
A heaven whose calm is ne'er o'ercast.'

*But none saith where is my Maker who giveth
songs in the night?*

How insupportable would be the days, if the
night, with its dews and darkness, did not come to
restore the drooping world! As the shades begin
to gather around us, our primeval instincts are
aroused, and we steal forth from our lairs, like the
inhabitants of the jungle, in search of those silent
and brooding thoughts which are the natural prey
of the intellect.—THOREAU.

In thy lone and long night-watches, sky above and wave below,
Thou didst learn a higher wisdom than the babbling schoolmen
 know,
God's stars and silence taught thee, as His angels only can,
That the one, sole, sacred thing beneath the cope of heaven is
 man.   —WHITTIER.

Attentive, and with more delighted ear,
Divine Instructor, I have heard, that when
Cherubic songs by night from neighboring hills
Aerial music send.   —MILTON.

Oh, sirs, there are moments in the history of men
and of nations, when they stand so near the vail
that separates mortals from immortals, men from
their God, that they can almost hear the beating
and feel the pulsations of the heart of the Infinite.
   —GARFIELD.

31. *Of such an one will I glory: yet of myself will I not glory, but in mine infirmities.*

The intent of prophecy. *But as for Me, this secret is not revealed for wisdom that I have more than any living, but for their sakes. And no man taketh this honor to himself, but he that is called of God.*

'Trust not in thine own knowledge, nor in the subtlety of any living creature, but rather in the grace of God, who helpeth the humble and humbleth those that be self-presuming.'

For who maketh thee to differ, and what hast thou that thou didst not receive? Now we have received not the spirit of the world, but the spirit which is of God—which things we speak, not in the words which man's wisdom teacheth, but which the Holy Ghost teacheth.

That I may discern between good and bad.

God left Hezekiah to try him, that He might know all that was within his heart in the business of the ambassadors of the princes of Babylon, who sent unto him to inquire of the wonder that was done in the land. Hezekiah rendered not again according to the benefit, for his heart was lifted up.

'O Pride! the primal cause of all our woe.'

Cowper to Mrs. Cowper in London. Though my friend, you may suppose, before I was admitted an inmate here, was satisfied that I was not a mere vagabond, and has since that time received more convincing proof of my *sponsibility*, yet I could not resist the opportunity of furnishing him with ocular demonstration of it, by introducing him to one of my most splendid connexions; that when he hears me called that *fellow Cowper*, which has happened heretofore, he may be able, upon unquestionable evidence, to assert my gentlemanhood, and relieve me of the weight of that opprobrious appellation. Oh pride! pride! it deceives with the subtlety of a serpent, and seems to walk erect, though it crawls upon the earth. How will it twist and twine itself about, to get from under the cross, which it is the glory of our Christian calling to be able to bear with patience and good-will.

'1· *Behold my family is poor in Manasseh, and I am the least in my father's house.*

> Oh mountain climbers, ye will fail
> The starry stairs to see!
> For heaven lies nearest that sweet vale—
> A child's humility.'

2. *Study to show thyself approved unto God, a workman that needeth not to be ashamed, rightly dividing the word of truth.*

He must keep the sacred treasure a distinct thing from the earthen vessel in which God has placed it, and while he faithfully presents the treasure, let him leave it submissive to his Master whether men shall honor or dash the vessel that contains it.—HICKOK.

Cursed be he that doeth the work of the Lord deceitfully.

The happiness of the world is the concern of Him who is the Lord and Proprietor of it, nor do we know what we are about, when we endeavor to promote the good of mankind in any ways but those which he has directed, that is, in all ways not contrary to veracity and justice. I speak thus upon supposition of persons really endeavoring, in some sort, to do good without regard to these. But the truth seems to be, that such supposed endeavors proceed almost always from 'ambition, the spirit of party, or some indirect principle, concealed perhaps in great measure from persons themselves.—BUTLER.

'We are willing to pay a price coined out of our hearts for the coronation of our hearts, but seldom are we willing to suffer for others.'

3. *Depart ye, depart ye, go ye out from thence, touch no unclean thing, go ye out of the midst of her, be ye clean that bear the vessels of the Lord. Prepare thine heart and stretch out thine hands toward Him.*

> ' The best obedience of our hands
> Dares not appear before His throne.'

Thou neither seest thy original nor actual infirmities: but hast such an opinion of thyself, and of what thou doest, as plainly renders thee to be one that did never see a necessity of Christ's personal righteousness to justify thee before God.

Ignorance.—What! you are a man for revelations! I believe that what you and the rest of you say about that matter is but the fruit of distracted brains.

Hopeful.—Why, man, Christ is so hid in God from the natural apprehensions of all flesh, that He cannot by any man be savingly known, unless God the Father reveals Him to them first. Also, when we think that all our righteousness stinks in His nostrils, and that therefore He ·cannot abide to see us stand before Him in any confidence even of all our best performances.—BUNYAN.

4. *Follow on to know the Lord.*

Venture with courage and faith on untried explorations, like Columbus in search of a new continent.—J. L. T.

And yet I show unto you a more excellent way. Beware lest any man spoil you through philosophy and vain deceit, after the tradition of men, after the rudiments of the world, and not after Christ.

Thrice unhappy world, that takes Dryasdust's reading of the ways of God.—CARLYLE.

Henceforth call we no man master. Loose thyself from the bands of thy neck, O captive daughter of Zion. Stand fast in the liberty wherewith Christ has made us free.

Henceforward I am the truths. I will have no covenants but proximities. I appeal from your customs. I will not hide my tastes or aversions, I will so trust what is deep is holy, that I will do strongly before the sun and moon, whatever may rejoice me and the heart appoints.—EMERSON.

5. *For the Lord God spake thus to me with strong hand and instructed me, that I should not walk in the way of this people—neither fear ye their fear, nor be afraid. Sanctify the Lord of hosts Himself, and He shall be for a sanctuary.*

'Endeavor to know God's will by studying His word, observing His providence, and considering the promptings of His spirit within you when asking counsel at the throne of grace, and having ascertained His will with reference to His service, do it at all hazards and at any sacrifice.'

> A hand! A cloud formed hand!
> The hand God's chosen find,
> Always revealed to point before,
> When God is close behind.

Sound appreciation and just decision as to all the objects that come round about you; and the habit of behaving with justice and wisdom. Rarely should a man speak at all unless it is to say that thing that is to be done, and let him go and do his part in it and say no more about it.—CARLYLE.

6. *O Timothy, keep that which is committed to thy trust, avoiding profane and vain babblings and oppositions of science falsely so called.*

'It must gird itself to the sublimest task that the intellect has ever yet proposed:—to organize the comprehensive results of the world's thinking and co-ordinate the varied and fragmentary truths of research into one grand organon of principles, that

shall be a faithful reflex of the verity of things;
that shall combine the authenticity of science with
the full breadth of nature, and become a guiding and
trusting light to man through the vicissitudes of his
earthly experience. In the din and chaos of sects
and parties, in the confusion of doctrines and conflict of opinions, amid the gropings of despondency
and the exaltations of hope, we yearn for the voice
of nature, for the consolations and encouragements
of a philosophy which has the divine warrant of
accordance with the realities of the universe.'

7. They brought him to the startling brink,
   But he in fear recoiled :
   And none was found to try the depth—
   The day's high sport was spoiled.

   At length, a thought broke on his mind,
   His face lit up with hope ;   ·
   I'll venture down the rocks, he cried,
   If father holds the rope.

   Down, down, that awful depth of rock
   The father held his boy,
   While he his bosom filled with flowers,
   'Mid rapturous shouts of joy.

   Down clouds and mists our Father lets
   His chain of promises;
   And from His holy height He draws
   His children to the skies.

   O child of earth! with fear appalled,
   When oft thy path is cleft;

Though hanging on the abyss of doom,
Be not of hope bereft.

Whate'er His voice commands thee do
Nor count the sacrifice;
Go where the many dare not go,—
Pluck flowrets for the skies.

Our Father holds the rope, Amen!
The rocks are deep below:
But fearless we will swing and work,
Till heaven our trophies show.

8. *I shall be anointed with fresh oil.*

The interpreter answered, the fire is the work of
grace that is wrought in the heart; he that casts
water upon it, is the devil; but in that thou seest
the fire notwithstanding, burn higher and hotter,
thou shalt also see the reason of that. So he had
him about to the back of the wall where he saw a
man with a vessel of oil in his hand, of the which he
did continually cast, but secretly into the fire.—
BUNYAN.

*Thou, therefore, my son be strong in the grace that
is in Christ Jesus.*

Confide in His love, avail yourself of His power,
and demean yourself worthy of so precious a relation.—WINSLOW.

9. *Always delivered unto death for Jesus' sake.*
While we look not at the things which are seen.

Moses germinated in the solitude of the wilderness
when he lay in the grave of selfishness for forty long

weary years. Here in the garb of a vagrant Arab,
away from all the royal luxuries in which he had
been brought up, he obtained his glorious idea, 'I
shall redeem this people at last.' And, by virtue of
the inspiration thereof, he showed himself at the
court of Egypt again, as the veritable ambassador of
God come to emancipate a nation of slaves, and ultimately 'led his people' out of the land of the oppressor just as miraculously as Luther delivered the
Germans from papal power. . . Hence Moses must
have passed from the outward to the inward. Where
else could he have obtained this omnipotent wand?
Not certainly in dominions of sense. . . Can we not
say that conscience and reason always point a moni-
tory finger to the right place for us to fall into the
ground and die; to the place where, how great soever
the outward adversity, true happiness flows into our
being, as new life and joy flow into the bulb that lies
buried in the cold but creative earth? But this,
people are not far advanced enough to realize. They
persist to their detriment, in remaining on the surface of life, where they are ultimately destroyed by
the pleasant but baneful influences that induced
them to prefer it to the redemptive soil beneath—
erroneously founding their hopes of happiness on
their sensuous experiences, they take the appearance
for the reality; and as this mistake involves a loss
of the object in the method, hence arises all their
misery. . . But this state of affairs will always be,

3

until people fall into the ground and dying there, re-produce themselves in new glory, as the men they worship have done—fall into the dark but beneficial soil of self-denial, where they alone can germinate into the higher life in God, wherein the entire race is destined to dwell at last, freed from the inimical influences that conspire to prevent them from crossing its threshold.—LEPPER.

Do thou, O Lord, assist me against all worldly wisdom and understanding; do this, thou *must* do it, thou alone! It is not indeed my cause, but thine own. Come, oh come, I am ready even to give up my life patiently, like a lamb, for the cause is just: it is thine, and I will not depart from thee eternally. This I resolve in thy name. The world cannot force my conscience; and should my body be destroyed therein, my soul is thine, and remaineth with thee forever.—LUTHER.

Of my own will did I offer myself unto God the Father, for thy sins; my hands being stretched forth on the cross, and my body laid bare, so that nothing remained in me that was not wholly turned into a sacrifice for the appeasing of the divine Majesty. . . But if thou dost not offer up thyself freely unto my will, thy oblation is not entire, neither will there be perfect union between us.—KEMPIS.

'And faith has still its Olivet, and love its Galilee.'

10. I know thy burden, child; I shaped it,
  Poised it in mine own hand, made no proportion
  In its weight to thine unaided strength;
  For ever as I laid it on, I said
  I shall be near, and while she leans on me
  This burden shall be mine, not hers.

          —MESSENGER.

To each duty performed there is assigned a degree of mental peace and high consciousness of honorable exertion corresponding to the difficulty of the task accomplished. That rest of the body which succeeds to hard and industrious toil is not to be compared to the repose which the spirit enjoys under similar circumstances.—W. SCOTT.

He found himself in some sort compelled to undertake a work from which he shrank, and for which he felt no special aptitude. The nature of the work made him draw back. He was called upon to write the life of one whom he had known intimately, had loved and honored. It requires no sacrifice of feeling to analyze most minutely the character of one's imaginary hero. There the intellect feels no restraint; but to grope about in the heart of a dead friend, no matter how pure one may feel it to be, creates a revulsion of feeling. Yet the analysis must be made, and happily for him, with his interest in psychology, there existed a continual restraint upon a mere prying intellectualism in the reverence which he felt for the dead. . . In writing the lives of eminent Christians, biographers made the mistake of treating religion as the end to be attained, instead of a vital power at work in the soul. Indeed, he added, the very failure which you affirm of this class of writings demonstrates the high place in art which this class occupies. The easiest life.to write is that which is most outward. A life of adventure is the lowest form of biography. The hardest life to write is that which demands a record because of its strong character, and the highest form of biography is that which undertakes to display character through a representation of those forms which in actual life best contain and exhibit it. And what order of character presents to the biographer more glorious opportunities and greater perplexities than that which displays a new force revolutionizing it? The meshes of a man's inner life are not easy to trace, and when the great Weaver is busy in weaving the excellent pattern of Christ, the task of tracing becomes more difficult, healthy, instructive, yet very interesting. ... Novelists suffer their characters to work out their own destiny. Why should not biography borrow the same aid, and taking the life of some person quite unknown to fame, but having a strongly marked character, set forth the growth of that character under its changing experience of life; sketching with such fullness as need be, the world of nature and society, in which it moved, and showing how it was renewed and sanctified by Divine grace? In fact, beginning with chiseling a figure in basso relievo, our·friend proceeded to execute it in alto relievo, and finally constructed a detached statue. Nor was he unmindful of what may be called the proportions of breadth. The character has its whimsical side, but if that be unduly dwelt upon for the sake of making the general effect light and agreeable, the result may be to produce unjust contempt: so a cheerful mouth may from the painter's over anxiety to preserve the cheerful lines, be made to express a repulsive smirk. All this care could easily be fatal to success, unless he secured the presence of a still higher element, more intelligible than these. It was necessary that throughout his work, the shadow of the man himself should some how rest upon it—life-likeness, which cannot be super imposed, nor interposed, but supposed, the most elusive element to be reached after. The rest could in some sort be attained by study and carefully won, but this lay outside of any special effort and was rather the reward of patient labor in other directions. He possessed the more valuable aid of an affectionate enthusiasm for his subject.—The world does not want exact lines in the portraits of its hero's face, nearly so much as warm life which can make it believe in the existence of a common nature. To the biographer there fell rewards he had not anticipated—more absorbing in interest. At first he tried to escape from it, oppressed by this constant visitor. He fled for relief to other pursuits, and distracting entertainments, until he became reconciled

to the constant presence and found it a quiet joy.—
Much to live with a good man day after day, think
of his character, though, indeed, it often utters its
silent reproof:—to inquire into his source of power,
and to be so at one with him, that for a time you
have also the same earnestness of purpose, thrilled
with the same enthusiasm, and go with him through
the scenes which tried his soul, as if you were under-
going the same experience. The oblique light, too,
which our friend's study cast on other matters which
interested him, was often more valuable than the
direct rays. Indeed, there seemed to him no other
study, except the study of the life of Christ, which
was so productive as the life of one man. You live,
he would say, for months in the company of a single
person; you are let into the secrets of his life which
only he and you may know; you analyze his life,
and reconstruct it in your memorial, and by all this
study you get a deeper insight into the human heart
than would be possible by any general study of classes
of men, or movements; an history far deeper certainly, than it is possible to get, through mere familiarity with many living faces. But when all is done,
when you have tried to fathom this one man's heart,
you know that you have only troubled the waters
with your lead, that deeper than any plummet of the
human intellect can sound, lie depths of the soul;
and you arise from your task with new conceptions
of the worth of humanity, and profounder views of

that redemption which was so costly because the ruin was so great.—NEW ENGLANDER.

I could inform the dullest author how he might write an interesting book. Let him relate the events of his own life with honesty, not disguising the feelings which accompanied them. I never yet read even a Methodist's experience in the Gospel Messenger without instruction; and I should almost despair of that man who could peruse the Life of John Woodman without amelioration of heart.

—COLERIDGE.

12. My life, if I may judge by the decline of mental accuracy, has got more than half-way, and the rest is down hill. The half-way house is behind: and if Brighton be another form of Cheltenham, home cannot be very far off. I am getting tired. And the complexion of my spontaneous thoughts now, is increasing the contemplation of rest. Rest in God and love. Deep repose in that still country where the mystery of this strange life is solved, and the most feverish heart lays down its load at last.

—ROBERTSON.

People were solemnly warned against him. Those who knew little of his doctrines and less of himself, attacked him openly with an apparently motiveless bitterness. He had dared to be singular, and that in itself was revolutionary.—BROOKE.

' There runs a record that not only saith
    He loved his own, but loved them to the end;

So evermore a man shall love his friend,
    With friendship that outliveth life and death.'

*Wherefore, then, were ye not afraid to speak
against my servant Moses?*

13. ' See there! for this man, too, life's toil is over,
        His words are all said out, his deeds are done:
    For this man, too, there comes a rest, however
        Unquiet passed his time beneath the sun.

You said what seemed you best; your life's poor fountain
    Just bubbled; while his soared or shuddered down.
You chid him, as a tired boy chides a mountain;
    You frowned on him, and thought God too must frown.

His worst thought was so great, your best so little,
    Your best and worst not yours; his all his own.
You ran the world's safe way; he dared to thwart it.
    You stood with thousands by you—he alone.

Therefore, when God shall judge the world, I take it,
    He will not mete this man by rule and line;
Who felt no common thirst, nor feared to slake it
    From that which flowed within him—the divine.

O, think you God loves our tame-leveled acres
    More than the proud ditch of some heaven-kissed hill,
Man's straight-dug ditch, more than his own free river
    That wanders, he regarding, where it will?

Enough: high words abate no jot or tittle
    Of what, while man still lasts shall still be true,
Heaven's great ones must be slandered by earth's little,
    And God makes no ado.

Take heed you treat him well, forget it not,
    Look not upon him with disdainful eyes,
For though just now he seems of lowly lot,
    He is a prince, believe me, in disguise.

His title is secure, it cannot fail;
    His realm is wise, and as a garden fair.
The sweetest odors float on every gale,
    The brightest rivers flow and murmur there.

He does not seem of rank or wealth possessed,
    A poor unlettered man he meets you now,
But soon a star will glitter on his breast,—
    A golden crown will rest upon his brow.

He often walks among you; treat him well,
    This heir-apparent in a beggar's guise,
Lest, looking up, you meet displeasure fell
    Flashing upon you from a Father's eyes.

What though his garb is often poor and mean,
    He wears upon his hand a signet ring,
And goes attended by a guard unseen,
    Fit guard for one whose Father is a King.'

Lent.—Whether or not periodical self-denial in matters of common comfort conduce to form the true Christian, is a proper question for churches to decide. It is a question, however, on which they disagree. It is strenuously maintained, on the one hand, that such temporary abstinences increase the power to withstand temptation to really sinful indulgence— that they are to the Christian what his daily drill and constant target practice are to the soldier. On

3*

the other hand it is urged, that our sins so beset us, that there is no need of sham-fighting and target shooting to learn the art of Christian warfare—that this setting up of straw devils to shoot at, when the real article is so very convenient, indicates anything but a true appreciation of the condition of fallen humanity. While, however, we admit that the matter of self-denial comes fairly within the juris-diction of the divine, we must insist that the matter of diet belongs as exclusively to the physician. The machinery of the human system is so delicate and complex that the best of them tinker at its disorders as clumsily as a blacksmith would tinker a watch. Nevertheless they do know something of their business.

In the evil days of the later Roman Empire, and of the semi-pagan Christianity that satisfied the low intelligence of the times, Asceticism borrowed, among other heathen notions, the idea that the devil in us could be starved and flagellated out of exist-ence. They mistook the decline of vitality for a real ' conquest over the flesh.'

It is not for us to say what is appropriate diet for other countries, but when the lineal successors of St. Simon Stylites begin to tamper with the New England stomach, they lay their clumsy hands on a very delicate matter. Our digestion is our weakest point. Physicians tell us that the New Englander inclines too little to solid food, and too much to pastry and confectionery. Why not demand abstinence from them and not from meat? A forty days general abstinence from intoxicating drinks would go far to empty our jails and station-houses. Then continue the fast 325 days longer, and you would have the blessedest year America ever saw. How much also of the emigrants hard-earned money is perverted into tobacco? Would not a forty days' abstinence from this filthiness show substantial results?—HICKOX.

> The trials that those men do meet withal,
> That are obedient to the heavenly call,
>   Are manifold and suited to the flesh.
> O let the Pilgrims, let the Pilgrims, then
> Be vigilant, and quit themselves like men.
>
> —BUNYAN.

Hitherto there have been these two classes, renunciants and drunken devotees,—those on the one hand who descend into the plain, and are full soon down-bore - and destroyed: those on the other, who know no safety but by deprecation and flight. But the constructive soul must come: the mediator living and doing in the world, showing power, conquest among men, but not of them; translating into life, hallowing all the relations. Long time it must take to realize this gospel everywhere, in the gold market, the hustings, sanctifying trade, house-keeping, Wall street, Washington: but it is written in the leaf of destiny. There can and there will be mingling without degradation, love that shall be worship, chastened and sober, battle that shall be strength and perpetual victory.—MILLS.

King Henry's Penance. Ranulfus de Glanville, with a body of horse, in which were about four hundred knights, after a hard day's march, arrived at Newcastle. There he was told that William the Lion, instead of repressing, encouraged the devastation committed by the marauders, and, believing that there was no longer any army to face him, entirely neglected all the usual precautions of military discipline. The gallant sheriff resolved to push forward next morning in the hope of relieving Alnwick, and surprising the besiegers. The English accordingly began their march at break of day, and, though loaded with heavy armor, in five hours had proceeded nearly thirty miles from Newcastle. As they were then traversing a wild heath among the Cheviot Hills, they were enveloped in a thick fog, and the advice was given that they should try to find their way back to Newcastle; but Glanville, rather than stain his character with the infamy of such a flight, resolved to proceed at all hazards, and his men gallantly followed him. They proceeded some miles in darkness, being guided by a mountain stream, which they thought must conduct them to the level country. Suddenly the mist dispersed, and they saw before them in near view the castle of Alnwick beleaguered by straggling bands of Scots, and the Scottish King amidst a small troop of horsemen diverting himself with the exercises of chivalry, free from any apprehensions of danger. William at first mistook the English for a party of his own countrymen returning loaded with the sports of a foray. Perceiving his error, he was undismayed, and calling out, 'Noo it will be seen whilk be true knichts,' he instantly charged the enemy. In a few minutes he was overpowered, unhorsed, and made prisoner. Some of his nobles coming to the rescue, and finding their efforts ineffectual, voluntarily threw themselves into the hands of the English, that they might be partakers in the calamity of their sovereign. It so happened that the same hour at which William was taken at Alnwick, Henry had been doing penance at the tomb of St. Thomas of Canterbury. Alarmed by the dangers which surrounded him from domestic and foreign enemies, and dreading that he had offended Heaven by the rash words he had spoken, which led to the martyrdom of the Archbishop, he had thought it necessary to visit the shrine of the new saint. At the distance of three miles, discovering the towers of Canterbury Cathedral, he alighted from his horse and walked thither barefoot, over a road covered with rough and sharp stones, which so wounded his feet that in many places they were stained with his blood. His bare back was then scourged at his own request by all the monks of the convent, and he continued a whole day and night before the tomb, kneeling and lying prostrate on the hard pavement, employed in prayer, and without tasting nourishment. He then journeyed on to Westminster, and he was lying in bed very sick from the penance he had undergone, when, in the dead of night a messenger, stained with the soil of many counties, arrived at the palace, and declaring that he was the bearer of important dispatches, swore that he must see the king. The warder of the gate, and the page at the door of the bed-chamber in vain opposed his entrance, and, bursting in, he announced himself as the servant of Ranulfus de Glanville. The question being asked, 'Is all well with your master?' he answered, 'All is well, and he has now in his custody your enemy the King of Scots.' 'Repeat those words,' cried Henry in a transport of joy. The messenger repeated them, and delivered his dispatches. Henry having read them was eager to communicate the glad tidings to his courtiers, and, expressing gladness to Ranulfus de Glanville, piously remarked that the glorious event was to be ascribed to a higher power, for it happened while he was recumbent at the shrine of St. Thomas.—CAMPBELL'S CHIEF JUSTICES.

Dr. Johnson.—One morning afterwards when I found him alone, he communicated to me with solemn earnestness a very remarkable circumstance which had happened in the course of his illness, when he was much distressed by the dropsy. He had shut himself up and employed a day in particular exercises of religion—fasting, humiliation, and prayer. On a sudden, he obtained extraordinary relief, for which he looked up to heaven with grateful devotion. He made no direct inference from that fact, but from his manner of telling it, I could perceive that it appeared to him as something more than an incident in the common course of events.—BOSWELL.

16. ' Such wonders never come by chance,
     Nor can the winds such blessings blow.'

True, the salt seems in every instance to have been abstracted and locked up by accident; but the recurrence of the accident in every geologic formation, demonstrates it to be one of those on which the adept in the doctrine of chances might safely calculate. It seems an accident of the fixed class, on which Goldsmith bases his well-known reflection in the Vicar of Wakefield. ' To what a fortuitous concurrence do we not owe every pleasure and convenience of our lives! How many seeming accidents must unite before we can be clothed or fed! The peasant must be disposed to labor, the shower must fall, the wind fill the merchant's sail, or numbers must want the usual supply.—HUGH MILLER.

What can be more foolish than to think that all this rare fabric of heaven and earth could come together by chance, when all the skill of art is not able to make an oyster ?—TAYLOR.

So long as he sought the Lord, God made him to prosper.

I never lost my hope. I looked to the coming spring as full of responsibilities, but I had bodily strength and moral tone enough to look through them to the end. A trust based on experience as well as promises bouyed me up at the worst of times. Call it fatalism as you ignorantly may, there is that in the story of every eventful life, which teaches the inefficiency of human means, and the present control of a Supreme agency.—See how often relief has come at the moment of extremity, in forms strangely unsought, almost at the time unwelcome.—See still more how the back has been strengthened to its increasing burden, and the heart cheered by some conscious influence of an unseen Power.—KANE.

How hast thou helped him that is without power! How hast thou counseled him that hath no wisdom!

20. *And the Lord said unto him, Go through the midst of the city, through the midst of Jerusalem and set a mark upon the foreheads of the men that sigh and cry for all the abominations that be done in the midst thereof.*

For that righteous man dwelling among them, in seeing and hearing vexed his righteous soul from day to day.

To be where we and those around us are living in two different worlds of feeling, is tenfold more intolerable than to be where a foreign language, not one word of which we understand is spoken all day long. And if there be any part of our nature which is essentially human, and to effect the excision of which would destroy its humanity, it is the craving for sympathy.—ROBERTSON.

I often accuse my finest acquaintances of an immense frivolity. Several of them are decidedly pachydermatous. I say it in sorrow, not in anger. How can a man behold the light who has no answering light? They are true to their *sight*, but when they look this way they *see* nothing. For the children of light to contend with them is as if there should be a contest between eagles and owls. What stuff is that man made of who is not co-existent in our thought with the purest and subtlest truth? We select granite for the underpinning of our houses and barns; we build fences of stone; but we do not ourselves rest on an underpinning of granite truth, the lowest primitive rock:—we do not teach one another the lessons of honesty and sincerity that the brutes do, or of steadiness and solidity that the rocks do.—THOREAU.

> But while my sad bewildered view,
> The wide confusion vainly traces,
> One look I see serenely true,
> Amid the false and loveless faces.
>
> A voice not loud, like wind or wave,
> A look made low by conscious greatness,
> Where all is calm, and deep and grave,
> With a full soul's mature sedateness.

By His mild glance and sober power,
. Renewed to tranquil aspiration,
The sounds of surging riot cease.

—HYMNS OF A HERMIT.

21:     When the world appears apostate,
        And Love's labor all in vain,
        When I'm sick of sin and being,
        Struck with Doubt's most deadly pain, ·
        Tell me that there is no secret
        . In man's guilt or woe to thee:
        And with droppings of thy patience
        And thy peace, O quicken me.

The dejection I sometimes labor under, seems not to
rise from doubts of my acceptance with God, though
it tends to produce them; nor from desponding views
of my own backwardness in the divine life, for I am
more prone to dependence and self-conceit,—but from
the prospect of the difficulties I have to encounter in
the whole of my future life.   (His subsequent sufferings greater than he forsaw.)—Such a painful year
I never passed, owing to the privations I have been
called to on the one hand, and the spectacle before
me of human depravity on the other.   But I hope I
have not come to this seat of Satan in vain.—HENRY
MARTYN.

4. We have been proclaiming the Gospel in the
Burman Empire, with China on one side and India
on the other; Bhud and his monstrous fables de-
ceiving 400,000 on our right; and Brahma with his
metaphysical atheism chaining down 100,000 on our

left; whilst the base imposter Mohammed, rages against the Deity and Sacrifice of the blessed Saviour in the midst of both, with 10,000 or 20,000 of followers. But our Divine Lord shall ere long reign, and Bhuddist and Brahmanist, and Mohammedan—yea, the infidel and papist, and nominal Christian throughout Asia shall unite in adoring his cross.—BISHOP WILSON.

If you count all the growths of civilization for centuries, man is greatly superior to the animal. But what a condition of the world is that in which if you should destroy half its population, there would not be missed one treasure, one impulse, or one aspiration!—BEECHER.

Lord, when saw we thee an hungered?

'Oh, you who buy and sell cotton in New York, and are changers of money there and merchants beyond the seas; and you who float softly over carpets in palatial rooms and bridge over spaces in easy duties with music and the languid culture of the Arts'—

An English gentleman is generally highly educated. Society consists of cultivated persons, male and female, whose accomplishments are not displayed, but exist as a matter of course, and as essential to one's part in the duties and civilities of life. No one ventures to feel better informed than his neighbors, and hence there is a general deference to other men's opinions, and a reserve in expressing one's own which

is highly significant of extreme civilization and refinement.   Such a state of society, however, has its
drawbacks.   Character often becomes neutralized,
and genius itself dulled and flattened, when to distinguish one's self is felt to be an impropriety, and
where the manifestation of decided thought or feeling would be eccentric and even rude.   Hence, I observed a sort of uniformity in manner and expression
which is sometimes depressing; and when upon some
private occasion I have discovered that the smooth,
quiet personage whom I had seen in the dull propriety in which the pressure of company had held
him like a single stone in an arch, was a man of
feeling, of taste, of varied information, and accurate
learning, I said to myself, what a lamentable waste
is here!   This man who should have been enriching
the world with his stores of erudition, and of reflection has never conceived of himself as having anything to impart, or by which his fellow men should
profit.   His accomplishments are like his fortune and
respectability—his mere personal qualifications for a
position in society, in which he is contented to move
merely without shining or dispensing anything more
than the genial warmth of good humor and benevolence.   There are thousands of such men in England; living and dying in the most exquisite relish
of social pleasures, and deriving daily satisfaction
from their own mental resources, but contributing
nothing to the increase of the world's intellectual

wealth, and never dreaming of their attainments as talents which they are bound to employ.. They live among educated men; knowledge is a drug in the market, and what have they to confer?—A. C. COXE.

He that withholdeth corn, the people shall curse him: but blessing shall be upon the head of him that selleth it.

King Henry to Wolsey.—
                              I presume,
   That as my hand hath opened bounty to you,
   My heart dropp'd love, my power rained honor more
   On you than any:—So your hand and heart,
   Your brain, and every function of your power,
   As 'twere in love's particular, be more
   To me, your friend, than any?
                    *   *   Nature never lends
   The smallest scruple of her excellence,
   But, like a thrifty goddess, she determines
   Herself the glory of a creditor,
   Both thanks and use.   —SHAKSPEARE.

I can measure the profitless non-observing routine of the past winter by my joy at this first break in upon its drudgery. God knows I had laid down for myself much experimental observation, and some lines of what I hoped would be valuable travel and search; but I am thankful that I am here, able to empty a slop-bucket 'or rub a scurvied leg. The moral value of this toilsome month to myself has been the lesson of sympathy it has taught me with the laboring man. The fatigue, and disgust, and secret trials of the overworked brain are bad enough, but not to me more severe than those which follow the sick and jaded body to a sleepless bed.— KANE.

Starvation Fever.—The revelation has startled clever editors who took it for granted that rapidly-increasing national wealth must necessarily remove the causes of destitution. If they would take a little more heed of what is going on around, they would know from facts and figures, collected by men in the public service, and published by order of the House of Commons, that privation and starvation are the normal state of the bulk of the working population.—LONDON SUN COR.

London Poor.—Depressed by the sight of so much misery, and uninventive of remedies for the evils that force themselves on my perception, I can do little more than recur to the idea already hinted (a deluge). So far as these children are concerned, at any rate, it would be a blessing to them. This heroic method of treating human maladies, moral and material, is certainly beyond the scope of man's discretionary rights, and probably will not be adopted by Divine Providence until the opportunity of milder reformation shall have been offered us again and again, through a series of future ages.— HAWTHORNE.

The cross is God's never-to-be-broken pledge, that the resources of infinite love are employed to undo the work of evil, and establish justice and truth among men. By that sign Human Faith mounts the chariot of conflict, of conquest, and of victory. Love is stronger than hate, and will win its way to every citadel of iniquity and prostrate it in the dust. This is the unwritten and therefore ineffaceable creed that keeps heart and hope in the bosom of humanity.—PORTER.

'Is not this a scandal when Lazarus is lying at the doors, and Dives is out in his carriage every day in the parks? Every man and woman who is a Christian has been sitting not once, but all his life at the table of God's love, feeding his intelligence, tastes, his immortal spirit. Let him care for those who are wandering in wretchedness.'

In every missionary field there is need not only of the most elevated piety, but of the highest force of intellect and the ripest fruits of scholarship. Go where you will, it would be difficult to find such a company of men as Goodell, Schauffler, Dwight, Hamlin, and Everett. They are whole-souled men and rejoice in their work with exceeding great joy.—STODDARD.

The best educated people and best bred people, other things being equal, are best qualified for usefulness in this enterprize (at Hilton Head).

One of Gen. Mitchell's first efforts was to build them houses to live in: and the new, clean tenements at Hilton Head, looming up like a young, western village, are a monument to-day of his

promptness and energy :—trivial monuments to the
naked eye, bright and enduring to the thinking
heart. They are but the shadowy forerunners of
days to come, even as the first log huts of the
pioneer shrine the possibilities of great states that
lie waiting but to spring into life and grandeur.

Science loses a bright star from its zenith—society
a brilliant member from its circles—humanity a
warm and tried friend; while Philanthropy may
well veil her face and weep, as for a son dutiful and
loyal.

Mr. BEECHER said :—A few had fallen, and among
them Mitchell, who died at his post with his armor
on: and fortunate, thrice fortunate was it that the
door of heaven opened to him, not among the stars
where he loved to wander, but among Christ's poor
and helpless disciples, whom he was beginning to
teach, inspire, instruct, defend. It might kindle
the imagination more if he had departed while
keeping nightly watch upon those glorious orbs,
passing as from glory to glory. But nobler, more
sublime was his going, who all the way from the
sepulchre to the throne of God, heard airy voices
saying,—'Inasmuch as ye have done it unto one ot
the least of these my brethren, ye have done it unto
me.' Rest! Thy sun arose, but forgot to set: it
went not down, but from very noon arose higher
into the unhorizoned heaven.

12. Secretary STANTON asked the Savannah blacks

in the name of the Republic—'What do you want for your people?'

What shall one then answer the messengers of the nation? That the Lord hath founded Zion and the poor of his people shall trust in it.

'The nation has, during the past year, made palpable progress toward a recognition of the great truth, that a wrong done to the humblest and most despised, is an injury and grievance to all: and that Liberty can be perfect for none, until there are Liberty and Justice for all.'

• Our government is a sun in the firmament of political freedom, which is destined to be the centre of an extended and glorious system. Whatever threatens to make that sun go out in darkness, threatens the myriads that are to live in its light, with the gloom of a night whose succeeding morning no man can foretell.—NEW ENGLANDER.

15. *Moreover all the chief of the priests and the people transgressed very much after all the abominations of the heathen, and polluted the House of the Lord, which he had hallowed in Jerusalem.*

And you shall see young people at the Lord's table on the Sabbath day, and, before the week is out, whirling in these indecent dances as freely as any worldling of them all. Is it right? Can it be right? 'But they like it.' Like it, do they? I have no doubt the children of Israel liked the Golden Calf, but Moses ground it to powder. Mischiefs come in insidiously; they may need to be thrust out at the point of the bayonet. . . 'But then,' say some, 'we may as well give up society.' It may be. There are various forms of self-denial, and precious little of it among some disciples in these days. Perhaps our Lord meant them when he talked of self-denial. Also when He said, ' He that forsaketh not all that he hath, cannot be disciple.' We in the west are beginning to think that something must be done to save the country. Something definite and positive. Once, long ago, they went and searched for the ' accursed thing.' We do not pretend that we have found the accursed thing. But all reforms must enter into particulars, and take up one thing at a time. Mere general exhortation does not touch anybody or anything.

Is there any line between the church and the world ?—ONEST.

Thus have ye said, O house of Israel, for I know the things that come into your minds every one of them. And that which cometh into your mind shall not be at all that ye say. We will be as the Heathen. Sanctify now yourselves, and sanctify the house of the Lord God of your fathers, and carry forth the filthiness out of the holy place.

Your true life lies in the realm of noble thought, of divine purposes, of holy perseverance ; in generous self-denial, and self-abnegation.—BEECHER.

LORD BYRON writes :—I date my first impressions

against religion from having witnessed how little its votaries were actuated by true Christian charity.

21. The Provençal historian affirms that the final truce between Richard and Saladin was concluded in a fair, flowery meadow near Mount Tabor, when Richard was so much charmed with the gallant bearing of the Prince of Miscreants—as Saladin is civilly termed in the crusading treaties—that he declared he would rather be the friend of that brave and honest pagan than the ally of the crafty Philip or the brutal Leopold.—MISS STRICKLAND.

'O Jesus, are these Thy Christians?' cried the Mahometan prince, when the Christians broke their league with him?

Wherefore, thus saith the Lord, As I live, surely mine oath which he has despised, and my covenant that he hath broken, even it will I recompense upon his own head.

> 'The sacrifices I require,
> Are hearts which love and zeal inspire,
> And vows with strictest care made good.'

Within ye are full of hypocrisy.

'Christ did not adroitly wind through the various forms of evil, meeting it with expedient silence. The forces of righteousness must upheave the immoral elements before it can settle them on its own sure foundations.'

30. Travel in Europe shows an American droll things, and some of the drollest among his own country people. I never could understand why

many **men** from the other side of the sea came abroad, since they bring only their bodies with them, leaving their minds in their absorbing business at home. Many women, I have recently discovered, visit Europe mainly for the purpose of extending their shopping expeditions. . . I have heard husbands and fathers groaning over their tribulations. In their excess of agony, knowing that I was yet spared, as they put it, they confided to me how, since they had set foot on European soil, they had been nothing more than express agents, forwarding parcels and boxes filled with their wives and daughters' purchases

Anxious to defend woman from all aspersions, whether just or unjust, I have intimated to the complainers that perhaps their conversation was not agreeable, and that the fair shoppers were willing to appear more devoted to ·¯ t form of feminine rights than they really were.

The men stoutly denied this, and they were right in their denial.

In the cars and on boats I have heard women who talked of nothing but the best places to buy things. Italy was not the region of natural beauty and the home of art. It was the land where cameos, corals, and mosaics could be purchased to advantage. Holland had no associations, but it had beautiful linens. Switzerland was Alpless, but the wood carvings were very pretty. Belgium had no

history, no school of art, no Rembrants, no Gerard
Dows, no Paul Potters; but it wove laces in whose
fine meshes a woman's soul might well be lost.—
BROWNE.

I heard, and they spake not aright.

Women rule over them.—Women love pretty
things, and make men waste life in getting pretty
things.—FELIX HOLT.

*The Lord will take away the bravery of their
tinkling ornaments, chains and bracelets.*

Women of intellect take to the *belles lettres* rather
than to science, and the most of reading women
delight their emotional nature with sensational
novels.—PATTERSON.

There is no real criticism in Mrs. Montagu's
essay on Shakspeare; none showing the beauty of
thought as founded on the workings of the human
heart.—JOHNSON.

'Women whose chief concern it is to dress according to fashion are not likely to interfere with the
graver concerns of life. Health and decorum are
sacrificed in modern drawing-rooms—Heaven only
knows why—to the Moloch, Fashion.'

*The vail is upon their heart,—when it shall turn
to the Lord the vail shall be taken away. Seeing
then that we have such hope we use great plainness
of speech.*

1.   A perfect woman—nobly planned
       To warn, to comfort, and command.

7*

She openeth her mouth with wisdom, and in her tongue is the law of kindness. She looketh well to the ways of her household and eateth not the bread of idleness.

What does cookery mean? It means the knowledge of Medea, and of Circe, and of Calypso, and of Helen, and of Rebekah, and of the Queen of Sheba. It means the knowledge of all fruits, and herbs, and balms, and a knowledge of all that is healing, and sweet in fields, and groves, and savory in meats; it means carefulness, and inventiveness, and watchfulness, and willingness, and readiness of appliance. It means the economy of your great grandmothers, and the science of modern chemists; it means much tasting, and no wasting; it means English thoroughness and French art, and Arabian hospitality, and it means in fine that you are to be perfectly and always ' ladies, loaf givers.'—TRIBUNE.

' Would that you ladies would say, Is not every child on earth in a real, in a spiritual sense, my own child, for it is my sister's child? She may not do her duty to it. Shall I not do it for her? Be a lady, and do such things as these. Let no lady neglect to do so.'

2. *Love of Nature.*

' A heart open to the whole noon of nature, and through all its brightness drinking in the smile of a present God.'

Eugenie De Guerin's Journal.—In its pages the sacredness of the inner life is preserved in all its fragile beauty. .She had learned to distinguish what fed the deep springs of her being from the storms and cloud-shadows that touched but the surface, hence the book is almost destitute of those outward every-day events which merely occupy or perplex, and is filled with thoughts of God, the wants and destiny of our natures, sentiments of friendship, and raptures over the beauty which, to her watchful, reverent eye existed even in the solitudes of ' La Cayla.' Every page of the book is hallowed and individualized by the light of faith. It was this that gave vitality to every moment, earnestness to every action. .It was faith which extracted from prayer that rapture whose utterance trembles in golden silence. To this celestial eye nature was transparent, and literature glowed beneath it with a light that not only informed but exalted.'

3. We had intended to say something of that illustrious group of which Elizabeth is the central figure—the dextrous Walsingham, the impetuous Oxford, the elegant Sackville, the all-accomplished Sidney; concerning Essex, the ornament of the court and of the camp, the model of chivalry, the munificent patron of genius, whose great virtues, great courage, great talents, the favor of his sovereign, the love of his countrymen—all that seemed to insure a happy and glorious life—led to

an early and ignominious death ; concerning Raleigh, the soldier, the sailor, the scholar, the courtier, the orator, the poet, the historian, the philosopher. . .

We had intended also to say something concerning the literature of that splendid period, and especially concerning those two incomparable men, the Prince of Poets and the Prince of Philosophers, who have made the Elizabethan age a more glorious and important era in the history of the human mind than the age of Pericles, of Augustus, or of Leo.— MACAULAY.

* * On such occasions the littleness of Elizabeth's character entirely disappeared, and the imperial majesty of her noble nature possessed her wholly.— FROUDE.

> Alas! the human mould's at fault·
> And still by turns it claims
> A nobleness that can exalt,
> A littleness that shames.   —SWAIN.

> O Eve, in evil hour thou dids't give ear
> To that false worm!   —MILTON.

10. 'Minds made giddy by a reckless pursuit of pleasure, or repressed into the narrow routine of mere money-getting for money's sake, need to be roused and educated to higher views and desires. It would be a slow work to bring all ranks from the very lowest up to the highest of philosophic culture, where familiar with what great men in all ages have taught they shall really pause, and reflect, and search out wisdom. Perhaps the best that can be

hoped in this way is, that as the years go on a
larger and larger number shall reach this lofty
stand-point, so as gradually to raise the tone of
popular belief and conduct.'

It may be easy to prove to the simplest mind that
virtue is the best policy, but it is not as easy to
secure that clear judgment which reaches right
decisions, and makes one strong against the plausible
gloss of evil influence. But while bad men, or weak,
blind women are liable to gain the ascendancy, they
can give in a single month all the improvements
that the wisdom of ages has accumulated to the
destroying hand of an uneducated rabble. The
world of progress has been wiped out again and
again by the bubbling over of the waters of a reckless mob from the ditches and sewers which no one
had cared to cleanse. And the world will always
be in danger of such a deluge as long as we do not
look more closely to the springs of human action.—
MRS. AREY.

We owe it to posterity not to suffer their dearest
inheritance to be destroyed. But, if it were possible
for us to be insensible of these sacred claims, there
is yet an obligation binding upon ourselves from
which nothing can acquit us: a personal interest
which we cannot surrender. To alienate even our
own rights would be a crime as much more enormous than suicide, as a life of civil security and
freedom is superior to a bare existence: and if life

be the bounty of Heaven we scornfully reject the
noblest part of the gift if we consent to surrender
that certain rule of living, without which the condition of human nature is not only miserable but
contemptible.—JUNIUS' LETTERS.

*Since the day that your fathers came forth out of
the land of Egypt unto this day I have even sent
unto you all my servants, the prophets, daily rising
up early and sending them.   Yet they hearkened not
unto me, nor inclined their ear, but hardened their
neck: they did worse than their fathers.*

' Human nature is so blinded by her own independence and self-confidence that when she is
interested it is impossible for the mind to disarm
her of her predilections.'

*None of the lepers but Naaman the Syrian
cleansed.*

Man is born like a wild ass' colt, and it is only
by a long training in trials and afflictions that he
is brought to submission or obedience.—BEECHER.

14. How mean a thing were man if there were not
that within him which is higher than himself— if he
could not master the illusions of sense and discern
the connections of events by a superior light which
comes from God!   He so shares the divine impulses,
that he has power to subject interested passions to
love of country, and personal ambition to the en-
noblement of man.   Not in vain has Lincoln lived,
for he has helped to make this Republic an example

of justice with no caste but the caste of humanity. The last day of his life beamed with sunshine, as he sent his friendly greeting to the men of the Rocky Mountains, and the Pacific slope ; as he contempla- ted the return of hundreds of thousands of soldiers to truitful industry ; as he welcomed in advance hun- dreds of thousands of emigrants from Europe, as his eye kindled with enthusiasm at the coming wealth of the nations.   And so with these thoughts for his country, he was removed from the toils and tempta- tions of his life and was at peace.—BANCROFT.

—At first the strange, cold, ashen look disap- pointed me.   But gradually much of the old expres- sion came back to that marked head, to those features, so individual, so powerful, and so manly.   You missed the dark, soft, benignant eyes ; but God's peace, not man's violence, seemed to have pressed down the weary lids into welcome rest.   There was a cloak of patient serenity and forgivingness about the face most touching and peculiar.   The hands seemed to have dropped into just such a tired posi- tion that I had seen them fall into in brief intervals of weary hand-shaking.   Yet he seemed to be graciously receiving us all, though so mutely, and with no token of welcome.   As I gazed around on that old Hall (Philadelphia) consecrated to freedom by one of the grandest events in our national history, I felt that the scene had other witnesses than we, than those armed watchers, than the passing multitude—the immortal shades of heroes and patriots—the great, tried souls of the young Republic, in whose ways he had fearlessly walked, into whose fellowship he had been received.—GRACE GREENWOOD.

In common with most people I had concluded that the presidential honor came to Mr. Lincoln without paving. When the Douglas and Lincoln contest was ended, the defeated man said to his partner: ' Billy I knew that I should miss the place when I competed for it. This defeat will make me President. He refused, in the interim, any proposition looking to the acceptance of any lesser office, and with the concurrence of his friends and family. At the same time he took no pains to precipitate his opportunity; rather like a man destined, sat more closely to study and vigilance. Read all the issues as they developed, and waited for his call. It came at last in a special invitation to speak at Cooper Institute. He felt intuitively that this was the Rubicon, and with a human thrill, paused and hesitated. The best lawyer in his state, the hero of a debate equivalent to a senatorship, with a mind too broad and grave for a mere gubernatorial place, and already by four years destiny and prepraation President of the United States, he went up to the post with a dignity and ease that made men stare, because they had not seen the steps he took upon the road.—Speaking thus among the associations of his working life, the years of Abraham Lincoln began to return in the vividness of their monotony bleak and unremunerated, hard and practical, full of patient walk down a road without a turning; brightened by dutifulness alone, pointed, but not cheered by wayside anecdote, and successful, not so much because he was sanguine himself, as because he rated not eminence and honor too high, or too difficult. When he found himself competing for the senatorship with the quickest, the least scrupulous, and the most flattered orator in the Union, he saw nothing odd or dramatic about it. His presidential opportunity surprised everybody but himself; not that he had self-conceit, but that he thought the office possible.—He never made a bid for the favor or forgiveness of history, but ruled the nation as if it were practicing law, and practiced law as if it were ruling the nation. This real greatness of mind, obliviousness of circumstances, ascending from a practice of $3,000 a year to $25,000 as if there were no contrast between them, giving Billy the permission to use the firm style as before, without a conscious poetic trait, yet even in absent moments looking very long away, pondering the distance of rewards, promises, vindications with a longing that was poetry.— TOWNSHEND.

He is an able man. Through all his plain and homely simplicity appears a sagacity that grapples on equal terms with the mightiest intellects, and moves on undismayed to the consummation of the most momentous events of any age. Leather needs a

polish. Baubles require a setting. But the true dia
mond needs none. If Mr. Lincoln were polished
we might doubt whether his polish had not impose
him upon us for more than he is really worth. If h
were an aristocrat, we had not mistaken his assump-
tion for ability.—TRIBUNE COR.

*I have raised him up in righteousness, and I wil
direct all his ways: he shall build my city, and he
shall let go my captives, not for price nor reward.*

' God takes time, seldom begins and finishes a work
by the same agent, or in the same generation. On
sows and another reaps. He employs a successio
till it draws near its consummation, then he raises up
some controlling spirit who finishes the work.'

We don't know who our angels are ; we know no
what has been ours till we weep for what we have
lost. While he lived nobody suspected Mr. Lincol
of being a great man. We did not even know how
we loved him, till he died and crape floated fro
every door. Where now in high places can we fin
a man so simply grand ? Where one who could b
trusted to use limitless power as he did, withou
thought of himself ? ' If I am God's instrument
He will never forsake the thing that he uses, but i
must accomplish his purpose,' I once heard him sa
in the hey-day of his power, with a humility an
sadness never to be forgotten.

What is greatness ? It is not intellect alone. I
is not moral and emotional quality only. It is

character compounded of both. It is wisdom, it is high thought; it is wide vision. It is magnanimity, it is mercy; it is love; it is gentleness and child-heartedness; it is supremacy to all littleness.—M. C. A.

> To sit in courts or high debate,
> And found the statutes of the state
> Upon the testament of God.
> Then, after Love controls the lands—
> At last—to enter worlds unseen,
> For earth beneath in order stands:
> Ages will keep his memory green.
>
> —WILLARD.

18. *Speak ye also unto the children of Israel, saying, Verily my Sabbaths ye shall keep: for it is a sign between me and you throughout your generations; that ye may know that I am the Lord that doth sanctify you.*

Two inestimable advantages Christianity has given us: first, the Sabbath, the jubilee of the whole world! whose light dawns welcome alike into the closet of the philosopher, into the garret of toil, and into prison cells; and everywhere suggests even to the vile, the dignity of spiritual being. And secondly, the institution of preaching,—the speech of man to men. . . What hinders that now everywhere, in pulpits, in lecture-rooms, in houses, in fields, wherever the invitation of men, or your own occasions lead you, you speak the very truth as your life and conscience reach it, and cheer the waiting,

fainting hearts of men with new hope and new revelation? Yourself a new-born bard of the Holy
Ghost. Cast behind you all conformity, and acquaint
men at first hand with Deity. Look to it, first and
only, that fashion, custom, authority, pleasure and
money are nothing to you,—are not bandages over
your eyes, that you cannot see—but live with the
privilege of the immeasurable mind.—EMERSON.

Not as pleasing men, but God.

The subjects of the pulpit have never been varied
from the day the Holy Spirit visibly descended on the
first advocates of the Gospel in tongues of fire.
They have immediate relation to that eternity, the
idea of which is the living soul of all poetry and art.
It is the province of the preacher of Christianity to
develop the connection between this world and the
next, to watch over the beginning of a course that
will endure forever, and to trace the broad shadows
cast from imperishable realities on the shifting
scenery of earth.—TALFOURD.

It is constantly to remind mankind of what mankind is constantly forgetting; not to supply the de-
fects of human intelligence, but to fortify the feeble-
ness of human resolutions; to recall mankind from
the by-paths where they turn, into the path of salvation which all know, but few tread.—SYDNEY SMITH.

' It should be warm, a living altar-coal to melt the
icy heart and charm the soul.'

' It is in **the** sacred vessels of the temple that **the** oil of joy is kept, which God's people are to have for mourning.'

24. *Being predestinated according to the purpose of him who worketh all things after the counsel of His own will.*

Regarded from a human point of view, the possibility of apostasy remains· still for every regenerate man, upon every grade of development, even the highest; that is, the new man may be thrust aside by the old ; but just as decidedly we must say, that regarded from the Divine point of view, it is impossible for the elect of God to be overpowered by sin. Were it possible with one, it would be so with all, and then God's plans would be dependent on man's fidelity.—OLSHAUSEN.

That He might make known the riches of His glory on the vessels of mercy.

As the eyes of the company wandered from one piece to another of this rare assemblage, they observed in one corner of the apartment, the broken fragments of a vase, of which enough remained to discover that it had been intended to excel every other vessel in the room, being embellished with an uncommon ·profusion of ornaments, and emblazoned with the richest purple, scarlet and gold, besides many softer tints of violet, azure and rose color. After gazing sometime on the ruins of 'this splendid vessel, the whole company turned a look of inquiry upon the person who attended them, and who was

8*

also the conductor of the works; when he informed them that the vase had once promised fair to adorn the palace of the king. ' We lately undertook,' said he; ' to make two vases of that description, upon which it was determined that our utmost skill should be exerted, in order to give them the highest possible perfection of form, coloring and design. and indeed,' added he, ' this manufactory never produced more exquisite specimens of our art. The royal vessels had passed much to our satisfaction, through every other part of the necessary process, but upon being submitted to the trying operation of the last fire, one of them only came forth with increased beauty, while the other, probably from some flaw in its original constitution, was reduced to the fragments now before you.' . . Known unto God are all His works from the beginning; so that what He once destines to honor can by no means fall short of its appointed end. And to prevent all distressing doubts on this subject, our Omnipotent Former and Fashioner hath been graciously pleased to assure us that He will be with us in the furnace, upholding, strengthening and carrying us through every refining process, until He has placed us in a state of everlasting security. Hence it is said of the great God that His *work is perfect.* But the work of the human potter must needs partake of the fallibility of the hand that formed it.—Mrs. Sherwood.

Thy builders have perfected thy beauty.

Man, when he reaches the bloom of his *glorified* life, will unspeakably excel the angels in glory. His superiority lies in his capability of development. When the diamond is once disturbed by the ray of a burning reflector it is irrecoverably gone ; so are the angels once fallen, forever lost, according to the doctrine of Scripture. The rose can with difficulty be hurt, and even from its root it will send forth new life ; so was man rendered capable of entering into full spiritual life-fellowship with God through the help of his Saviour.—OLSHAUSEN.

Saved : Yet so as by fire.

To conclude this wretched story, the poor Doctor of Divinity, having been robbed of all his money in this little airing beyond the limits of propriety, was easily persuaded to give up the intended tour, and return to his bereaved flock, who, very probably, were thereafter conscious of an increased unction in his soul-stirring eloquence, without suspecting the awful depths into which their pastor had dived in quest of it. His voice is now silent. I leave it to members of his own profession to decide whether it was better for him thus to sin outright, and so be let into the miserable secret of what manner of man he was, or to have gone through life outwardly unspotted, making the first discovery of his latent evil at the judgment seat. It has occurred to me that his dire calamity, as both he and I regarded it, might have been the only method by which precisely such a man as himself, and so situated, could be redeemed. He has learned, ere now, how that matter stood.—HAWTHORNE.

> Out, damned spot!
> > Being unprepared,
> Our will became the servant to defect.
> > > —MACBETH.

Men fall often from a want of moral richness and moral culture into vices which are to the heart what vermin are to the soil.—BEECHER.

Men may rise on stepping-stones of their dead selves to higher things.—TENNYSON.

Whatever I have seen of the world, or known of the history of mankind, teaches me to look on the errors of others in sorrow, not in anger. When I take the history of but one poor heart that has sinned and suffered; when I represent to myself the struggles and temptations through which it has passed, the vicissitudes of hope and fear, the pressure of want, the desertion of friends, the scorn of a world that hath little charity, the desolation of the mind's sanctuary, the threatening voices within it, health gone, happiness gone, perhaps even hope, that remains the longest, gone—I would fain lay the soul of my fellow-being in His hand from whom it came.—CHALMERS.

> ' The miserable have no other medicine,
> But only hope.'

25. *Yet many a year didst Thou forbear them,
and testifiedst against them by Thy spirit in Thy
prophets; yet they would not give ear. Nevertheless,
for Thy great mercies' sake Thou didst not utterly
consume them, for Thou art a gracious and merciful
God.*

' All souls are Thine; the wings of morning bear
None from that Presence which is everywhere;
Nor hell itself can hide, for Thou art there.
Through sins, perversities of will,
Through doubt and pain, through guilt, and shame, and ill,
Thy pitying eye is on Thy creature still,
And Thou canst make eternal Source and Goal
In Thy long years, life's broken circle whole;
And change to praise the cry of the lost soul.'

Who can hear the terrors of the Lord of Hosts
without being awed into a veneration? Or who can
hear the kind and endearing accents of a merciful
Father and not be softened into love toward Him?

—SPECTATOR.

28. *Thou hast made the earth to tremble.*

The pillars of heaven's starry roof,
Tremble and start at His reproof.
But, if Thy saints deserve rebuke,
Thou hast a gentler rod.

*Israel hath cast off the thing that is good: the
enemy shall pursue him.*

*O vine of Sibmah! I will weep for thee with the
weeping of Jozer.*

Thus tenderly does God deal with Moabites,
much more with His own people.—HENRY.

'Yea, though his sins should dim each spark of **love**,
I measure not my love by his returns;
And though the stripes I send to bring him home
Should serve to drive him farther from my arms,
Still he is mine, I lured him from the world;
He has no home, no right but in my love.
Though earth and hell combined against him rise,
I'm bound to rescue him, for we are one.'

    'Here everlasting love displays
    The choicest of her stores.'

The saddest symptom of degeneracy I find in my nature is that base ingratitude of heart which renders me so unaffected by Thine astonishing compassion.—MASON.

Want of tenderness, Dr. Johnson always alleged, was want of parts, and no less a proof of stupidity than depravity.

Which things the angels desire to look into.

We bow down to the earth, and study and grovel in it, and content ourselves with the outside of the unsearchable riches of Christ, and look not within it: but they having no desire but for the glory of God, being pure flames of fire, burning only with love to Him, are no less delighted than amazed with the bottomless wonders of His wisdom and goodness, shining in the work of our redemption. It is our shame and folly that we lose ourselves and our thoughts in poor childish things, and trifle away our days we know not how, and let these rich mysteries lie unregarded.—LEIGHTON.

O, the love of Christ! the love of Christ! he (Dr. Judson) would suddenly exclaim, while his eye kindled, and the tears chased each other down his cheeks : we cannot understand it now, but what a beautiful theme for eternity!

11. The wood I walk in on this mild May day, with the yellow brown foliage of the oaks between me and the blue sky, the white star-flowers, and the blue-eyed speedwell, and the ground ivy at my feet— what grove of tropic palms, what strange ferns, or splendid broad-petaled blossoms could ever thrill such deep and delicate fibres within me as this home scene? These familiar flowers, these well-remembered bird notes; this sky, with its fitful brightness, these furrowed and grassy fields, each with a sort of personality given to it by the capricious hedge rows. Such things as these are the mother tongue of our imagination, the language that is laden with all the subtle, inexplicable associations the fleeting hours of our childhood left behind them. Our delight in the sunshine on the deep-bladed grass to-day might be no more than the faint perception of wearied souls if it were not for the sunshine and the grass of far-off years which still live in us, and transform our perception into love.—MILL ON THE FLOSS.

> Oft hae I rov'd by bonny Doon,
>   To see the rose and woodbine twine,
> And ilka bird sang o' its luve,
>   And fondly sae did I o' mine.　　　—BURNS.

What a noble gift to man are the forests! The winds of heaven seem to linger amid these balmy branches, and the sunshine falls like a blessing upon the green leaves; the wild breath of the forest, fragrant with bark and berry, fans the brow with grateful freshness, and the beautiful wood-light, neither garish nor gloomy, full of calm and peaceful influences, sheds repose over the spirit. Every object here has a deeper merit than our wonder can fathom; each has a beauty beyond our full perception.—MISS COOPER.

As to the town itself, I do not know whether I told you how much I nauseate it, but no length of time will ever cure my loathing of it. But sweet Nature! I have conversed with her with inexpressible luxury. A flower, a bird, a tree, a fly, has been enough to kindle a delightful train of ideas and emotions, and sometimes to elevate the mind to sublime conceptions.—FOSTER.

> A little last year's nest
>   Hangs gray and bare on yonder tree:
> No play of wind-tossed branches, drest
>   In blossom, hides the sight from me.
>
> Where are its hopes insphered in pearl—
>   Its downy life, so frail and fair?
> Love's welcome note—the hasty swirl
>   Of mother-pinions through the air?
>
> Poor nest! deserted, desolate,
>   The minister of deeds out grown:

Some subtle kinship with thy fate,
  The weary human heart may own!

Yet, stay! with short and sudden flight,
  Swift sidelong glance and airy rest;
A bird, amid the blossoms white,
  Alights beside the empty nest.

Her heart on building cares intent,
  With bright, quick-eyed and dextrous bill,
She gathers from the hoard unspent
  Materials for her loving skill.

In some far nook, concealed from view,
  Leaf-guarded from the noon-day glare,
The old nest, woven with the new,
  Shall serve life's purpose, fresh and fair.

I take the lesson to my heart,
  Sweet symbol of a truth divine:
Labor and love have larger part
  Than present use in man's design.

Each fearless word, each lifted cross
  Shall be the future's heritage;
Transition is not rest or loss:
  True deeds pass on from age to age.

                    —Miss Humphrey.

'The crickets sing a song of hope fulfilled, and though in that glad music there be neither speech nor language which we can recognize as such, there is yet a voice to be heard among them by all who love to listen with reverent delight to the sweet harmonies and deep analogies of nature.'

5

The providence that's in a watchful state
Knows almost every grain of Plutus' gold,
Finds bottom in th' uncomprehensive deeps,
Keeps pace with thought, and almost like the gods,
Does thoughts unveil in their dumb cradles.

—Shaks.

And made him friends of mountains; with the stars
And the quick spirit of the Universe
He held his dialogues; and they did teach
To him the magic of their mysteries:
To him the book of night was opened wide.
And voices from the deep abyss revealed
A marvel and a secret.—Byron.

22. This is a dreadful state of things that is declared by Dr. Schwabe, president of the statistical
board at Berlin, to exist in that intelligent city.
Children, he says, though much improved by public
instruction, 'are strangely deficient in the knowledge
of Nature and natural phenomena. From about
1,000 children examined before being admitted into
school, 777 never saw any rainbow, 633 a field of
potatoes, 602 a butterfly, 583 the sunset, 462 the
rising of the sun, 460 a meadow, 406 a corn field,
387 a flock of sheep, 364 a forest, 264 an oak tree,
and, lastly, 167 had never heard the song of the lark.'
No wonder this statement made, as is reported, 'a
great sensation.' What prospect of a happy or useful life to children brought up amid all the advantages
of a great city, and yet ignorant of so simple things

as ' corn fields,' and ' flocks of sheep,' and ' the song of the lark,' and all the rest.—INDEPENDENT.

The whole force of education, until very lately, has been directed in every possible way to the destruction of the love of nature. The only knowledge which has been considered essential among us, is that of words, and the next after it, of the abstract sciences; while every liking shown by children for simple, natural history, has been either violently checked (if it took an inconvenient form for the house maid), or else scrupulously limited to hours of play; so that those who can thus use their eyes and fingers are for the most part neglected or rebellious lads, while your well-behaved and amiable scholars are disciplined into blindness and palsy of half their faculties. Herein there is a notable ground of difference between the lovers of nature and its despisers. We shall find that the love of nature has been a faithful and sacred element of human feeling—that is to say, supposing all circumstances otherwise the same with respect to two individuals; the one who loves nature most, will be *always* found to have more *faith in God* than the other. It is intensely difficult, owing to the confusing and counter influences which always mingle in the data of the problem to make this abstraction fairly; but so far as we can do it, so far, I boldly assert, the result is constantly the same; the nature-worship will be found to bring with it such a sense of the presence and power of a Great Spirit as no mere reasoning can either induce or controvert; and where that nature-worship is innocently pursued —*i. e.*, with due respect to other claims on time, feeling, and exertion, and associated with the higher principles of religion,—it becomes the channel of certain sacred truths, which by no other means can be conveyed. The greater number of the words which are recorded in Scripture, as directly spoken to men by the lips of the Deity, are either simple revelations of His law or special threatenings, commands and promises relating to special events. But two passages of God's speaking, one in the Old and one in the New Testament, possess, it seems to me, a different character from any of the rest having been uttered; the one to effect the last necessary change in the mind of a man whose piety was in other respects perfect; and the other, as the first statement to all men of the principles of Christianity by Christ himself.—I mean the ·38th to 41st chapters of the book of Job, and the Sermon on the Mount. Now, the first of these passages is from beginning to end nothing else than a direction of the mind to the works of God in nature. And the other consists only in the inculcation of *three* things: first, right conduct; second, looking for eternal life; third, trusting God, through watchfulness of His dealings with His creation. As far as I can judge of the ways of men, it seems to me that the simplest and most necessary truths are always the last believed; and I suppose that well-meaning people in general would rather regulate their conduct and creed by almost any other portion of Scripture whatsoever, than by that Sermon on the Mount.—RUSKIN.

1. *Take this child away and nurse it for me and I will give thee thy wages.—Certainly I will be with thee.*

A cruel adversary intends the destruction of them all. Nature frames for them an ark of bulrushes, and leaves them to waves and winds, and monsters prowling for what they may destroy. Temptations will assail them. Troubles will overtake them. Death will claim them. You have to fortify them against vice and tribulation. You have to qualify them, if your education of them is adapted to their condition in this world, not only to live but also to die. Picture to yourselves the ministering spirits clothing them with the 'white robes,' placing upon their heads the crowns of glory, and putting into their hands the golden harps on which they are to strike before the throne the strains of celestial gladness. The everlasting Father seals their investiture, and bids them follow the Lamb whithersoever He goeth. I say unto you that He will in some shape or other give you your reward.—DEHON.

As for me this is my covenant with them, saith the Lord. My spirit that is upon thee, and my words which I have put in thy mouth shall not depart out of the mouth of thy seed and out of the mouth of thy seed's seed from henceforth and forever.

It is our business to do all the preparatory work— to perform all that human agency allied to divine power can accomplish, and then, with a sublime and cheerful faith, to leave to God the developing process. We may not take you into the dark room of His purposes and counsels and providences; but it is His work to develop and impress His own image upon the heart you have so patiently trained and cultivated, and in His own good time the work shall be done.— WENDELL.

For precept must be upon precept, precept upon precept.

We are all envious naturally, but by checking envy we get the better of it. So we are all thieves naturally; a child always tries to get what it wants the nearest way. By good instruction and good habits this is cured, till a man has not even an inclination to seize what is anothers; has no struggle with himself about it.—JOHNSON.

The disposition to hate evil is one of the benefits of the old catechetical instructions. A man that follows his impulses gains in some respects, but if those impulses are not directed and regulated by definite doctrinal and ethical views and by definite conventional usages, their spontaneity tends to vagueness, and to a condition in which all qualities mingle and form a mixture, the individual elements of which are all lost.'

More precious than fine gold.

Yesterday, I took my leave of J. I put him on board his boat, and he and I parted with words and thoughts too deep for tears, as Wordsworth wrote. God bless him! If I were a beggar on a dung hill, it ought to be riches to me to have such a son. He is pious, without an ounce of affectation, a genuine child of God's own sonship. He has very good abilities, good health, good habits, cool judgment, calculation, forethought, with an amount of fearlessness which surprises. He is laborious, modest, self-denying, conscientious to the last scruple. Dear fellow! he loves you all with the sincerest love, and I came back to my club, feeling that I had parted with a treasure. God is with him.—HAVELOCK.

We brought nothing into this world.

' In the Science of Life we must all begin for ourselves where our great-grandparents began. Just as morning will bring with it the same sequence of morning, noon, and night that dawned, and flamed, and faded in Eden.'

' What, you may ask, should be the moral education you ought to give your sons? My answer is, that you would not comprehend it if you have not yourself experienced its routine. Acquire and you will then be enabled to confer it?'

Man was meant to grow up amidst nature, and all the activities of human society. His senses were meant to be avenues through which the Divine order and beauty of the material world were to be opened to his inner being, to stir into sympathy and life a corresponding spiritual order and beauty there. It was meant that he should grow up under the influences of home and society,—under a mother's love and father's wisdom, and amidst the kind deeds of brothers, sisters, friends: and so through all this finite love and wisdom rise to the worship of the Infinite Heart, and the Absolute Wisdom. It was meant that he should grow up in this adventurous school of human society, with its varied enterprises, contests, and experiences; be put at the risk of limb and life, and come, under the captaincy of conscience, into conflict with error, ignorance, and wrong, and grapple with them; and so by struggle and victory rise to the comprehension of the supreme power there is in the Absolute Truth and Integrity, that are the elements of the universe. As our physical capacities and instincts appear — some earlier, some later, just when occasion calls for them—so these higher spiritual capacities and instincts unfold themselves just when and where the need for them appears. God does not burden us with knowledge before we have a use for it, but by a beautiful law, the very need when it comes touches some hidden spring, and lo, the curtain is drawn aside, and the very truth we want stands there revealed. No sooner, for instance, is a child capable of going wrong, than his inward vision is opened to the superior loveliness of the right, and his sense of moral obligation vitalized to bind him to the better course. And thus it is through the whole course of life. At every need, at every emergency, at every cry of the heart, God reveals himself just so far as the occasion demands, and his child can comprehend and profit.—POTTER.

> ' Each filial cry shall find a Father near,—
> A faithful friend to love, to bless, to save.'

We must break away the blackened ligatures that bind the cramped spirit; we must stir the tremulous threads of feeling into life: we must place them where the airs are like the airs of home to them; where the murmur of pure fountains will teach them faith and trust in God and in humanity, and the heart of the child will blossom like the silver lilies, whose every glimpse is beauty, and every motion a delight.—MRS. AREY.

Culture cannot begin too early. In talking with scholars, I observe that they lost on ruder companions those years of boyhood which alone could give imaginative literature a religious quality in their esteem.

The secret of culture is to learn that a few great points steadily reappear, alike in the poverty of the obscurest farm and in the miscellany of metropolitan life, and that these few alone are to be regarded :— the escape from all false ties, courage to be what we are; and love of what is simple and beautiful ; independence and cheerful relation : these are the essentials—these and the wish to serve—to add somewhat to the well-being of man.—EMERSON.

In the midst of a lesson his cold and calm voice would fall upon me in the midst of a demonstration. ' No ! ' I hesitated, stopped, and then went back to the beginning, and on reaching the same spot, ' No ! ' uttered with the tone of perfect conviction, barred my progress. ' The next ! ' and I sat down in red confusion. He, too, was stopped with ' No ! ' but went right on, finished, and, as he sat down was rewarded with ' Very well.' ' Why,' whimpered I, ' I recited it just as he did, and you said, No ! ' ' Why didn't you say Yes, and stick to it ? It is not enough to know your lesson ; you must know that you know it. You have learned nothing till you are sure. If all the world says No, your business is to say Yes, and prove it.' It was tough for a green boy, but it seasoned him.—BEECHER.

When they shall be hungry they shall fret.

It sounds extreme to say that a child should never be allowed to express a dislike of anything which cannot be helped.

The race of grumblers would soon die out if all children were so trained that never, between the ages of five and twelve did they utter a needless complaint without being gently reminded that it was foolish and disagreeable.—H. H.

'A constant succession of little contemptible worries tends to fasten a querulous, grumbling disposition, such as renders a man a nuisance to himself, and to those about him. To meet great misfortunes we gather up our endurance, and pray for Divine support and guidance; but as for small blisters—the insect cares of daily life—we are very ready to think that they are too little to trouble the Almighty with them, or even to call up our fortitude to face them.'

13. *He that killeth an ox as if he slew a man: he that sacrificeth a lamb as if he cut off a dog's neck: he that offereth an oblation as if he blessed an idol.*

'Inward brutality cannot be disguised even in sanctimony; more offensive and provoking.'

For if the woman be not covered, let her also be shorn; but if it be a shame for a woman to be shorn or shaven let her be covered.

'Outward sign of an inward grace.' Wanting in that respect to themselves and others which indicates a high degree of moral purity and virtue.

And he made as though he would have gone further. But they constrained him, saying, Abide with us.

Christ was a matchless model of delicacy and true reserve. He had the fullness and the majesty of those qualities which come from an unsullied divine

love. It must needs be that He should be invited,
though He overshadowed them in the stature of His
being transcendently greater; for that very reason
he respected their individuality, and the smallest
heart-rights that belonged to any one of them. And
when you stand in heaven you will see the amplifi-
cation of that in God. Not one taste or feeling that
belongs to you that God will not respect with the
utmost delicacy, for His greatness is not like ours,
tumultuous and undiscriminating, but respecting and
respectful. As soon as Christ saw that they wanted
Him, then He wanted them. And is not that love
all the world over?—reserved and standing upon its
right and dignity, and maintaining power and control over itself, so long as it thinks itself not wanted:
but the moment it perceives that it is wanted—free,
frank, discursive, and overflowing.—BEECHER.

A man's behavior to his inferiors is the surest
test of his breeding. Be pitiful, be courteous, con-
descend to men of low estate, are maxims of
Christianity, the justice of which is acknowledged
by the highest civilization.—TRIBUNE.

If we know ourselves we shall remember the
condescension, benignity, and love due to inferiors
—the affability, friendship, and kindness we ought
to show to equals—the regard, deference, and honor
we owe to superiors—and the candor, integrity, and
benevolence we owe to all.—MASON.

Their whole demeanor was easy and natural, with

that lofty grace and noble frankness which bespeak
free-born souls that have never been checked in their
growth by feelings of inferiority. There is a healthful hardiness about real dignity that never dreads
contact and communion with others, however
humble. You were only reminded of the difference
of rank by the habitual respect of the peasant.—
IRVING.

The integrity of Diogenes, without his churlish-
ness, and as his wisdom was useful to him, so it
rendered him agreeable to the rest of the world.

The immortal Prince Eugene, who, glorious from
his courage, and amiable from his clemency, is yet
less distinguished by his rank than his politeness.

Want of attention, not want of capacity, that
leaves us so many brutes.—CHESTERFIELD.

21. We read of people 'who have the scale of
your whole nervous system, and can play all the
gamut of your sensibilities in semi-tones—touching
the naked nerve pulps as a pianist strikes the keys
of his instrument.' We read that there are as great
masters of this nerve playing as Vieuxtemps or
Thalberg in their lines of performance.

O! At that sudden exclamation the child who was
taking her music lesson paused, with her fingers on
the piano keys and asked, 'What's the matter Miss
Macauley? Did I strike a wrong key?' Agnes Macauley did not answer. There was a wrong key
struck elsewhere than on the piano, and she was

looking straight at the visitor in Mrs. John Vincent's parlor door. It was a gentleman who came directly forward with a smile that wreathed his whole face. Agnes Macauley thought involuntarily of Carker in 'Dombey and Son,' Carker with his broad smile and gleaming teeth. 'This is an unexpected pleasure, Miss Macauley,' was the greeting between the shining rows of teeth. If he had been Vieuxtemps or Thalberg he could not have felt more pleasure at a sight of a grand instrument with magnificent compass and delicacy of tone. Agnes Macauley shivered. It was the premonitory sign of the delicacy of her organization, and then with a command of herself that showed her power of will, coolly said, 'How do you do, Mr. Bailey?' ''I never was better,' answered the gentleman. 'My voyage has quite cured me of that old affection of the heart, or lungs, or liver, that used to trouble me, and I flatter myself I am perfect picture of health. I see music has its ol charm for you.' Agnes Macauley made brief de nial. 'I see you are devoted to the piano still in spite of your indifference,' the gentleman continued as if his first touch had failed to strike the real re sponsive chord. 'Yes,' Agnes Macauley answered in a proud, defiant way, 'I am devoted to the pian as washer-women to their tubs, and seamstresses t their needles. They are the tools wherewith we earn our daily bread.' The man had struck the righ chord now. Jerome Bailey had made Agnes Ma

cauley confess to him that she was a music teacher.
Jerome Bailey shifted his touch like a musician test-
ing the compass of an instrument. 'I suppose I will
find your mother and sisters at the old place?' he
remarked. 'The old place has passed into strangers'
hands, and my mother and sisters have gone West,'
Agnes Macauley answered in a voice that suggested a
moan down deep in the springs of her life. 'Ah,'
Jerome Bailey exclaimed, as if he were hearing the
news for the first time. Agnes Macauley knew better.
She began to pick at the ends of the crimson sash,
thrown carelessly around her shoulders to protect her
from the chill of Mrs. John Vincent's grand parlors.
Jerome Bailey smiled at the movement. If he had
been Vieuxtemps or Thalberg, he had not smiled
more at the vibration of the keys after his fingers
had left them.'—Harper's Weekly.

Mr. Gladstone is known to be a sensitive man, who
feels keenly any personal attacks : and small enemies
naturally delight in teasing with their petty but
venomous darts, a noble adversary who shows that
he is galled by every touch. Such men find no profit
in attacking Bright, who is as imperturbable as ada-
mant or Ajax : and when he does strike back, always
crushes his enemy with the supreme calmness of a
confident strength, which cannot be irritated. Therefore, all the resources of malice have been exhausted
to wound Mr. Gladstone. The utmost recesses of
his private life have not been held sacred ; his re-

ligious faith, his dealings as a citizen, his sources of income, everything connected with his character as a citizen, his dealings as a citizen, his sources of income, everything connected with his character as a statesman, a husband, a father, and a gentleman, his enemies have scrutinized and ransacked to find an excuse for calumny. Finding none, they have slandered without excuse and without shame.'

'General Scott returned home in 1848 to stand his trial before a court-martial on charges preferred against him by such creatures as ——, and to prosecute charges against other officers. His readiness to accept affront from the most insignificant persons of no sensitiveness to indignities which a more callous nature would never have noticed, enabled unworthy men in the army and in the government to wound him beyond bearing, and to goad him in the extremity of his sufferings, to retorts unbecoming his greatness.'

I am humiliated by the reflection that it is, (or was) in the power of such insects to annoy me.— GREELEY.

To bear evil-speaking and illiterate judgment with equanimity is the highest bravery. It is, in fact, the repose of mental courage.

To persecute the lover of truth, for opposing established customs, and to censure him in after ages for not having been more strenuous in opposition, are errors which will never cease, until the pleasure of self-elevation from the depression of superiority is no more.—MONTAGU.

Rid me out of the hand of strange children, whose mouth is full of vanity.

These hungry-eyed wretches who set in the unsuspicious circle of parents and children, treasuring their words, spying their weaknesses, misinterpreting the innocent liberties of the household, and then run from house to house with their shameless news, are worse than poisoners of wells, or burners of houses. They poison the faith of man in man. Greedy listening is as dishonorable as nimble tattling. The ear is the open market where the tongue sells its ill-gotten wares. Some there are, who will not repeat again what they hear, but they are willing to listen to it. They will not trade in contraband goods, but they will buy enough for family use! It is a shame to listen to ill of your neighbor. Christian benevolence demands that you do not love ill news. A clean heart and a true honor rejoice in kindly things. It should be a pain and sorrow to know of anything that degrades your neighbor in your eyes, even if he be your enemy.—BEECHER.

'When the rich carpet is stained, the fool pointeth to the stain; the wise man covers it with his mantle.'

'Many a wretch has riden on a hurdle who has done much less mischief than utterers of forged tales, coiners of scandal and clippers of reputation.'

23. *Say not, I will recompense evil.*

No man can be injured ultimately but by himself. HALL.

No good fame can help, no bad fame can hurt him. The Laws are his consolers, the good Laws themselves are alive; they know if he have kept them. EMERSON.

A weak mind would have sunk under sucn a ∟oa` of unpopularity. But that resolute spirit seemed to derive new firmness from the public hatred. The only effect which reproaches appeared to produce on him was to sour in some degree his naturally sweet temper.—MACAULAY.

With me it is a very small thing that I should be judged of you.

My ears are stone·deaf to this idle buzz, and my flesh is as insensible as iron to these petty stings. I have an invincible confidence that my poems will co-operate with the benign tendencies of human nature and society wherever found; and that they will in their degree be efficacious in making men wise, better and happier.—WORDSWORTH.

> I said to cold neglect and scorn,
> Pass on, I heed you not,
> Ye may pursue me till this form
> And being are forgot.
> But still the spirit which you see,
> Undaunted by your wiles.
> Draws from its own nobility
>   Its high-born smiles.

July 4.—Europe, the smallest in area of the continents, culminates in its centre into the icy masses of the Alps. From the glaciers, where all the great rivers have their sources, they descend the declivities and radiate to the different seas. The Danube flows directly east to the Pontic Sea; the Po, to the Adriatic; the Rhone, to the Sea of Lyons; the Rhine, north to the German Sea. Walled off by the Pyrenean and Carpathian Mountains, divergent and isolated, are the Tagus, the Elbe, and other single rivers, affluents of the Baltic, the Atlantic, the Mediterranean, and the Pontic Seas. Descending from common radiant points, and diverging every way from one another, no intercommunication exists among the rivers of Europe toward their sources; navigation is petty and feeble; art and commerce have never, during thirty centuries, united so many small valleys, remotely isolated by impenetrable barriers. Hence upon each river dwells a distinct people, differing from all the rest in race, language, religion, interests and habits. Though often politically amalgamated by conquest, they again relapse into fragments from innate geographical incoherence. .Religious creeds and diplomacy form no more enduring bond. The history of these nations is a story of perpetual war— of mutual extermination; an appalling dramatic catalogue of a few splendid tyrannies crushing multitudinous millions of submissive and unchron-

icled serfs. Exactly similar to Europe, though
grander in size of population, is Asia. From the
stupendous central barrier of the Himalayas run
the four great rivers of China, due east, to discharge
themselves under the rising sun. Toward the south
run the rivers of Cochin China, the Ganges, and the
Indus ; toward the west, the rivers of the Caspian ;
and north, through Siberia to the Arctic Sea, many
rivers of the first magnitude. During fifty centuries,
as now, the Alps and Himalaya Mountains have
proved insuperable barriers to the amalgamation of
the nations around their bases, and dwelling in the
valleys that radiate from their slopes. The continents of Africa and South America, as far as we are
familiar with the details of their surfaces, are even
more than these perplexed into dislocated fragments.

In contrast, the interior of North America presents toward heaven an expanded bowl, to receive
and fuse into harmony whatsoever enters within its
rim. So, each of the other continents presenting a
bowl reversed, scatter everything from a central
apex into radiant distraction. Political societies
and empires have in all ages conformed themselves
into these emphatic geographical facts. This demo-
cratic republican empire of North America is then
predestined to expand and fit itself to the continent ;
to control the oceans on either hand, and eventually
the continents beyond them. Much is uncertain,
yet, through all the vicissitudes of the future, this

much of eternal truth is discernible. In geography the antithesis of the old world, in society we are and will be the reverse. *Our* North America will rapidly accumulate to a population equaling that of the rest of the world combined : a people one and indivisible, identical in manners, language, customs, and impulses; preserving the same civilization, the same religion; imbued with the same opinions, and having the same political liberties. Of this we have two illustrations now under our eye, the one passing away, the other advancing. The aboriginal Indian race, amongst whom, from Darien to the Esquimaux, and from Florida to Vancouver's Island, exists a perfect identity in hair, complexion, features, religion, stature, and language; and second, in the instinctive fusion into one language and into one new race of immigrant Germans, English, Norwegians, Celts, and Italians, whose individualities are obliterated in a single generation. The possession of the Basin of the Mississippi, thus held in unity by the American people, is a supreme, a crowning mercy. Viewed also as the dominating part of the great calcareous plain formed of the conterminous Basins of the Mississippi, St. Lawrence, Hudson's Bay, and Mackenzie, the amphitheatre of the world; here is supremely, indeed, the most magnificent dwelling-place marked out by God for man's abode. Thus, the perpetuity and destiny of our sacred union find their conclusive proof and illustration in the bosom of nature. The political storms that periodically rage are but the clouds and sunshine that give variety to the atmosphere, and checker our history as we march. Behold, then, rising now and in the future, the empire which industry and self-government create. The growth of half a century, hewed out of the wilderness: its weapons, .the axe and plow; its tactics, labor and energy; its soldiers, free and equal citizens. Behold the oracular goal to which our eagles march, and whither the phalanx of our states and people moves harmoniously on, to plant a hundred states and consummate their civic greatness.—GILPIN.

10. In exhaustlessness and variety of resources no other country on the globe equals ours beyond the Mississippi. In grand natural curiosities and wonders all other countries combined fall far below it. Its mines, forests, and prairies await the capitalist. Its dusky races, earth-monuments, and ancient cities importune the antiquarian. Its cataracts, canyons, and crests woo the painter. Its mountains, minerals, and stupendous vegetable productions challenge the naturalist. Its air invites the invalid, healing the system wounded by ruder climates. Its society welcomes the immigrant, offering high interest upon his investment of money, brains or skill; and, if need be, generous obliviousness of errors past—a clean page to begin anew the record of his life. From the dim confines of Egypt

and China, has the spirit of Progress, like the fabled
one of Jewish legend doomed to no respite from his
wandering, marched on by Greece, Rome, and
Western Europe, across the Atlantic, through
Jamestown Harbor, over Plymouth Rock—on, on,
toward the serene Pacific. Ere long through the
Golden Gate of San Francisco it will go out by the
islands of the sea to that dreamy Orient where it
was born. And then what? Four-fifths of all
civilized nations, past and present, have lived within
the world-encircling belt between the 30th and 50th
parallels of north latitude. Our own day shows a
line of great cities—Baltimore, Cincinnati, St. Louis,
Chicago, Omaha, Leavenworth, Salt Lake, Virginia,
Nevada, and San Francisco—extending almost as
directly as the bird flies, across the broad continent.
Here run the grooves of Commerce, the routes of
travel, the pathway of empire.—A. D. RICHARDSON.

> 'From lake to gulf, from sea to sea,
>   Our country stands defined :
> Godlike, in that she dares to be
>   The friend of human kind !
>
> Of liberty, the gift of God,
>   She makes a common good ;
> And sees in all upon her sod
>   An equal brotherhood.'

*Thou shalt not abhor an Edomite, for he is thy
brother.*

I know not what record of sin awaits me in the

other world: but this I know, that I was never mean enough to despise any man because he was poor, or because he was ignorant, or because he was black.— Gov. Andrew.

'To judge properly of the negro you should see him educated, and treated with the respect due to a fellow-creature, uninsulted by the filthy aristocracy of the skin, and untarnished to the eye of the white by any associations connected with the state of slavery.'

'A Professor Axenfield, of Russian origin, recently appointed Professor of Medical Pathology at the College of Medicine in Paris, said in his inaugural speech, that the most glorious height to which a country could attain, was when she received every man, no matter how poor, or of whatever blood or race he might be, and gave him full and fair opportunities to work and achieve distinction, without regard to birth or rank.'

I thanked the overseer for his information, and bade him good day, and he touched his hat and the people all wished me a cheerful adieu. But I caught a few words from the overseer after my back was turned. It was not an order but sounded something like this : 'Hear ye people! The Herr is from America. Think ye once! It is forty times as far as Berlin, and he has come all the way here to see our Herr Oekomierath's famous farm.' Without any intention of correcting the latter's error, I unconsciously turned round and there they all stood. The old women were leaning upon their spades, the younger ones standing more erect, the children resting their baskets upon the ground; they had paused for a moment from their work, and there were forty pairs of eyes gazing intently upon a stranger from that land of which they had heard so much—a land where silver and meat and bread were plenty; the promised land of so many oppressed and poor and weary mortals—on this side of the great sea. And as I glanced upon that heterogeneous mass of faces—upon the heads covered with matted hair, some white with the frosts of many winters through which they had toiled with burdens along the chausées and thought of the suns of scores of summers of labor in the hovel, the field, the street, and stall, and upon others whose fresh, youthful curls were tied back with coarse, tow strings, and the freshness of their young lives, too, bound down by toil, yet good, kindly faces as they were— the thought came over me: 'And this is civilized Europe, and this the nineteenth century.' Then my eyes grew moist as I turned away once more; and there was a choking in my throat, and there came welling up within my soul a feeling of thankfulness to the Providence that had made me a citizen of that land for whose blessings these less favored ones longed so earnestly.—TRIBUNE COR.

Spanish women.—There are five thousand of them glad to work from morning till night, with their

babies in their arms, for less than enough to purchase
the barest necessities of life. The position of a con-
vict in an American State prison is so vastly better
than that occupied by these women of Seville, that it
seems a charity to wish them safely located in that
happy place. It is such scenes as these that makes
the American thank Providence for the inestimable
boon of his nationality. There are five thousand
women in San Francisco, happy wives and mothers,
with children that come home from public school five
days in a week, to find a table spread with food
known only to the rich in Europe, who owe the whole
difference in their condition to having been born in
America, and residing in San Francisco instead of
Seville. If they were here, they would be as likely
as not toiling in the tobacco house at twenty cents
per day with their half-starved children on their
knees. It is a good thing for those that labor to be
in our favored land, and they should never forget to
be thankful for it.—SWIFT.

The Jew.—Necessity has made him the master
alike of finance and commerce, and the nation that
has beaten him by hard blows into inaction or thrust
him out by persecution, has invariably come to grief
from the lack of those elements of prosperity which
he by gift and education knew how to create and
control. The history of Europe since the fourth
century is cumulative evidence of this fact. For
more than one thousand years the Jew was the scorn

of every civilized people and the spoil of every ruler. He was tortured upon the slightest pretense, and put to death on the slightest provocation. Laws gave him no protection. To be the owner of houses and lands, to freight his own ships, and pasture his own herds, only exposed his liberty and life to greater jeopardy. Money, or the equivalent of money that could be concealed till time of need and then used to bribe his oppressor, was his only power. Hence the knowledge of the value of coins, bullion, plate, and precious stones, gained by the terrible discipline of ages, and at the present day apparently, almost intuitive. The gold piece, no matter of what coinage; the diamond, no matter of what setting; the pearl and ruby and topaz and amethyst and emerald, whether prepared for the market or rough from the mine, are known to him instantly in their true value. In every nation the leading capitalist is a Jew. In every unsteady market, in every speculative monetary venture, in every critical occasion where tact and caution united to boldness and common sense are required on the instant, you find the Jew present.

As remarkable as the Rothschilds for wealth is their kinsman, Sir Moses Montefiore, for philanthropy. Taking into the account all his advantages of person, gifts, education, wealth, rank, and an age of eighty-seven years, by the unanimous voice of the European public, irrespective of race or religion, there is not the man living, not since John Howard died has the man lived, who has quietly and unostentatiously achieved so great results in the relief of suffering and righting of wrong as this noble English Jew.

In the matter of education the Jews in every country and every age have been careful and liberal. Intelligence is the marked feature of the race. In whatever class of society the Jew moves, he is never below its level.—DODGE.

Jewish Brethren.—If any one desires to revive his detestation of caste, the oppression of class by class, of color by color, of race by race, let him mark in the history of this people how *uniformly* they rise and expand and ennoble when the stigma is removed and the repressive laws are abolished. Always complying with the fundamental conditions of prosperous existence, that is, being always as a people chaste, temperate, industrious, and frugal, they have only needed a fair chance to develop more shining qualities. America can boast no better citizens, nor more refined circles than the good Jewish families of New York, Cincinnati, St. Louis, Philadelphia. . . Our Israelitish brethren in the United States have their own battle to fight. It is substantially the same as ours. They, too, have to deal with overwhelming masses of ignorance and poverty, just able to get across the ocean, and arriving helpless at Castle Garden. They too, have to save morality, decency, civilization, while the old bondage of doctrine and habit is gradually loosened. In this struggle Jews and Christians should be allies.—PARTON.

Evils.—In the speech of Mr. Gladstone in London, at the Lord Mayor's inauguration, the significant confession is made that: 'Whatever the tendencies of modern civilization—whatever its triumphs, they have not had, nor are they likely to have in our day or in our children's the effect of lightening the responsibilities of the Government.'

The United States affords evidence, in many portions of it, that our republican system is afflicted with such deep corruption as to produce the apprehensions which draw from the English premier his guarded but ominous admissions. The times call for wisdom, virtue, and prudence, there and here, or wide-spread confusion may follow.—CURTIS.

In thee have they set light by father and mother: in the midst of thee have they dealt by oppression with the stranger: in thee have they vexed the fatherless and the widow.

They have despised mine holy things and hast profaned my Sabbaths.

Who is there even among you that would shut the doors for nought? neither do ye kindle fire on mine altar for nought.

'Individuals will exist and be judged and recompensed in a future world: but bodies politic will have no future existence, and are therefore recompensed in this world.'

*Seventy years of Babylonish Captivity.—To fulfil
the word of the Lord by the mouth of Jeremiah, until
the land had enjoyed her sabbaths : for so long as she
lay desolate she kept Sabbath.*

'The penalty of Adam's stain hath descended
upon all mankind. The small power that remaineth,
is as it were a spark lying hid in the ashes. This is
natural reason itself, encompassed about with great
darkness, yet still retaining power to discern between
true and false, good and evil, although it be unable
to fulfil all that it approveth and enjoyeth no longer
the full light of the truth nor soundness of the affections.'

' O my brother ! lose not thy confidence of making
progress in godliness : there is yet time : the hour
is not yet past.'

*The good Lord pardon every one that prepareth his
heart to seek God, though he be not cleansed according to the purification of the sanctuary.*

17. Sin has changed the customs and habits of
men, corrupted their maxims, monopolized the use
of their property, absorbed their minds in vanity,
blinded their eyes, and corrupted their hearts. It is
the design of Christianity to eradicate all these evils,
and to restore to human nature its pristine beauty
and dignity. If once rightly applied it will purify
the heart of all its vileness, in spite of long established custom, or caste, or superstition, or an enthralling
system of priestcraft. Where then is the nation so

vile, that she may not be benefited by the gospel?
Is India that nation?—READ.

India.—'Young Wilson had applied himself so
closely to study during his whole college course, that
the approach of the final examination—an occasion of
so much alarm to the dissipated and idle—gave him
no particular uneasiness. He passed the trying or-
deal with great credit to himself and carried off the
prize for an English essay on Common Sense. It is an
interesting fact that when he descended the rostrum
Reginald Heber arose to recite his poem of Palestine.
There is something in the history of these two young
aspirants who were afterwards called to bear ' the heat
and burden of the day,' in the same distant field;
something also in the scrolls they held, characteristic
of the men—the one throwing over India the charm
of poetry, piety, and a loving spirit; the other stamp-
ing upon it the impress of Scriptural supremacy and
evangelical truth : something of adaptation also in
the ordering of those quiet spots where they rest in
their graves—the chancel of St. John's Trichino-
poly, and the chancel of St. Paul's Calcutta.'

Judson—' *A laborer with moral virtue girt.*'—' The
laborer has reached his field. It stretched out, a
wretched, sterile, neglected scene. . . To perform
the whole work of a pioneer missionary, in his peculiar sphere of labor, he must become an author in the
language, a popular preacher, a metaphysical rea-
soner, a translator of the Scriptures. · But for feeling

his way into the heart of a language, and following
out its innate principles of development, till the
whole structure stood in characteristic form before
his eye,—in this he has had few equals and probably
no superiors. It was not so much quickness as
method: the action of a mind naturally clear and
vigorous, but indebted, for its unerring precision and
force of movement, to his long course of severe intellectual training. Had he allowed himself, while
at school and college, to contract habits of superficial
study, or had he cut short the term of preparation
that he might hasten two or three years sooner to
the field of labor, how different would have been the
result! That familiarity with the general laws of
language, and with the genius of various languages
which he had derived from a critical study of the
classical and Hebrew tongues, were, in his case, what
Belzoni's researches among the labyrinths of Thebes
were to him, when he sat down before the blank wall
of the pyramid of Cephrenes, and reasoned out the
passage to its interior treasures. No time, after
arriving on missionary ground, was wasted in
blundering guesswork; every step he advanced
was taken once for all. Within three years after
entering Burmah, the man who had acquired his
first little stock of words by pointing to the common objects about him, and catching their names
from the lips of the natives, prepared a grammar
of the language, which must be reckoned among the

most remarkable productions in the field of philology.

He denied himself all English reading, except a single newspaper and a few books of devotion; relinquished so far as possible English society and correspondence; and sought by exclusive intercourse with the natives, and with the literature of the country, the power not merely of using the words of the language with facility, but of thinking and feeling, of living wholly in it. The result was, a style of composition in which his own strong mental characteristics spontaneously expressed themselves with all the freshness and force of one ' to the manor born.' His Burman Bible has been pronounced ' perfect as a literary work.' But its highest praise is in the fact, that it is free from all obscurity to the Burman mind. It must ever be, like Wickliffe's in the English, the basis and model of all others for the use of the people.—MRS. CONANT.

Lying here on my bed I have had such views of the loving condescension of Christ and the glories of heaven, as I believe are seldom granted to mortal man. It is not because I shrink from death that I wish to live, but a few years would not be missed from my eternity of bliss.—JUDSON.

From Clive's third visit to India dates the purity of the administration of our Eastern empire. He first made dauntless and unsparing war on that gigantic system of oppression, extortion, and corruption. In that war he manfully put to hazard his ease, his fame, and his splendid fortune. The same sense of justice which forbade us to conceal or extenuate the faults of his earlier days, compels us to admit that those faults were nobly repaired. If the reproach of the Company and of its servants has been taken away—if in India the yoke of foreign masters, elsewhere the heaviest of all yokes, has been found lighter than that of any native dynasty— if to that gang of public robbers which once spread terror through the whole plain of Bengal, has succeeded a body of functionaries not more highly distinguished by ability and diligence than by integrity, disinterestedness and public spirit—if we now see men like Munro, Elphinstone, and Metcalfe, after leading victorious armies, after making and deposing kings, return, proud of their honorable poverty, from a land which once held out to every greedy factor the hope of boundless wealth—the praise is in no small degree due to Clive. His name stands high on the roll of conquerors. But it is found on a better list—in the list of those who have done and suffered much for the happiness of mankind.—MACAULAY.

If difficulties try the powers of superior minds, Hastings, on assuming the government had a boundless field for the exercise of his talents in Bengal. Popular sufferings, disease and dilapidation, the result of a tremendous pestilence which had swept away a third of the people, suppressed all those energies which the cessation of war and the protecting spirit of a British government might have renewed. The treasury was almost empty—the revenues were sinking year by year ; the farmer, the traveller, and the merchant were rapidly disappearing, and in their place had come the robber and the tiger. Hastings applied himself vigorously to check this flood of evil, and he soon showed the value of practised experience and intellectual vigor in encountering the severest public privations. His first work was, to put down the lawlessness which had exposed life and property to constant violence ; and the bands of robbers, almost legalized by long impunity, found themselves, to their astonishment, suddenly made the objects of a vigorous police. The revenue system next came under his unhesitating hand. He rapidly purified its details and at once increased the amount of the public receipts, and diminished the expense of their collection. He next established District Courts, and so far, in principle, showed that justice might be brought to the doors of the population. Then, ascending to the higher machinery of the system, he divided the supreme council into committees, and by appointing intelligent and active superintendents in place of inefficient boards, gave the force of responsibility to office, and brought the whole apparatus of government into a condition to meet any emergency. And all this was the work of two years.—BLACKWOOD'S MAGAZINE.

30. *Mexico.*—'Maximilian alighted from the carriage as they reached the spot, and with careless grace brushing the dust from his garments, advanced toward the line of soldiers, and inquired who were to fire upon him. The platoon being pointed out, he gave to each of them a piece of gold, and requested them to aim well at his heart. He then approached M. and M., and embracing them three times with much fervor said: ' In a few moments we shall meet in another world.'—Advancing with admirable coolness, he said : ' Mexicans ! men of my class and my origin who are animated with my sentiments are destined by providence to make the happiness of people, or be their martyrs. When I came among you I did not bring with me illegitimate ideas. . . Before descending into the grave, I will add that I take with me the consolation of having done all the good in my power. . . May my blood be the last spilled, and may it regenerate Mexico, my unfortunate adopted country.'

A man of some real nobleness, this Albert, though not with wisdom enough, or good fortune enough could he have continued to rule the situation, to march the fanatical papistries and Kaiser Karl clear out of it and home to Spain and San Justo a little earlier, to wave the coming Jesuistries away as with a flaming sword, to forbid beforehand the Thirty Years' War, and the still dolefuler spiritual atrophy which has followed therefrom. He might have been

a German Cromwell beckoning his people to fly-eagle-like straight toward the sun, instead of screwing about in that sad, uncertain, and far too spiral a manner.
—CARLYLE.

7. *Total Eclipse of the Sun.*—The mighty pall of darkness hung over us for almost three minutes! At two minutes after five as we stood gazing at the black orb, with its magnificent corona, a sudden flash of golden light burst forth from the northern limb. It was the most thrilling instant I ever knew, and the most splendid spectacle I ever witnessed. As if God said: ' Let there be light,' a sheaf of dazzling rays burst forth in a twinkling and came flying toward us through the air. The whole sky lightened instantaneously.—CUYLER.

From Portsmouth to Oran to see the Eclipse.—The clouds and blue spaces fought for a time with varying success. The sun was hidden and revealed at intervals, hope oscillating in synchronism with the changes of the sky. At the moment of first contact a dense cloud intervened, but a minute or two afterwards the cloud had passed and the encroachment of the black body of the moon was evident upon the solar disc. The moon marched onward and I saw it at frequent intervals: a large group of spots were approached and swallowed up. Subsequently I caught sight of the lunar limb as it cut through the middle of a large spot. The spot was not to be distinguished from the moon, but rose like a mountain above it. The clouds, when thin, could be seen as grey scud drifting across the black surface of the moon: but they thickened more and more and made the intervals of clearness scantier. During these moments, I watched with an interest bordering upon fascination the march of the silver sickle of the sun across the field of the telescope. It was so sharp and so beautiful. No trace of the lunar limb could be observed beyond the sun's boundary. Here, indeed, it could only be relieved by the corona which was utterly cut off by the dark glass. The blackness of the moon beyond the sun was, in fact, confounded with the blackness of space. Beside me was Elliot with the watch and lantern, while Lieutenant Archer, of the royal engineers, had the kindness to take charge of my note-book. I mentioned, and he wrote rapidly down, such things as seemed worthy of remembrance. Thus my hands and mind were entirely free; but it was all to no purpose. A patch of sunlight fell and rested upon the landscape some miles away. It was the only illuminated spot within view. But to the northwest there was still a space of blue which might reach us in time. Within seven minutes of totality, another small space toward the zenith became very dark. The atmosphere was, as it were, on the brink of a precipice; it was charged with humidity, which required but a slight chill to bring it down in clouds. This was furnished by the withdrawal of the solar beams; the clouds did come down, covering up the space of blue on which our hopes had so long rested. I abandoned the telescope and walked to and fro like a leopard in its cage. As the moment of totality approached, the descent toward darkness was as obvious as a falling stone. I looked toward a distant ridge where I knew the darkness would first appear. At the moment a fan of beams issuing from the hidden sun, was spread out over the southern heavens. These beams are bars of alternate light and shade, produced in illuminated haze by the shadows of floating cloudlets of varying density. The beams are really parallel, but by an effect of perspective they appear divergent, like a fan, having the sun, in fact, for their point of intersection. The darkness took possession of the ridge to which I have referred, lowered upon M. Janssen's observatory, passed over the southern heavens, blotting out the beams as if a sponge had been drawn across them. It then took successive possession of three spaces of blue sky in the south-eastern atmosphere. I again looked toward the ridge. A glimmer as of day-dawn was behind it; and immediately afterwards the fan of beams which had been for two minutes absent revived in all its strength and splendor. The eclipse had ended, and as far as the corona was concerned we had been defeated.—TYNDALL.

12. *With clouds he covereth the light; and commandeth it not to shine by the cloud that cometh be-*

twixt. For he maketh small the drops of water; they pour down rain according to the vapor thereof; Which the clouds do drop and distil upon man abundantly.

Let us trace the progress of a single pint of the water thus elaborated from where it first alights on the spongy soil in a wintry shower, till where it sparkles in a glass in the pump room at Cheltenham. It falls among the flat hills that sweep around the ancient city of Worcester, and straightway buries itself, all fresh and soft in the folds of the Upper New Red Sandstone where they incline gently to the east. It percolates in its downward progress along one of the unworkable seams of rock-salt that occur in the superior marls in the formation; and as it pursues furlong after furlong its subterranean journey, savors more and more strongly of the company it keeps; becomes in succession hard, brackish, saline, briny; and then many fathoms below the level at which it had entered escapes from the saliferous stratum through a transverse fissure, into an inferior Liasic bed. And here it trickles for many hundred yards through a pyritiferous shale, on which its biting salts act so powerfully that it becomes strongly tinctured by the iron oxide and acidulated by the sulphur. And now it forces its upward way through the minute crevices of a dolomitic limestone, which its salts and acids serve partially to decompose, so that to its salt, iron and sulphur, it now adds its lime and its magnesia. And now it flows through beds of organic remains, animal and vegetable—now through a stratum of belemnites, and now a layer of fish—now besidea seam of lignite, and now along a vein of bitumen. Here it carries along with it a dilute infusion of what had been once the muscular tissue of a crocodile, and here the strainings of an ichthyosaurus. And now it comes gushing to the light in an upper Liasic stratum, considerably higher in the geologic scale, than the saliferous sandstones into which it had at first sunk, but considerably lower with reference to the existing levels. And now take it and drink it off at once, without pause or breathing space. It is not palatable, and it smells villianously, but never did apothecary mix up a more curiously compounded draught; and if it be not as salutary as it is elaborate, the faculty are sadly in error.

The art of deciphering the ancient hieroglyphics sculptured on the rocks of our country, is gradually extending from the few to the many. When the hard names of the science shall become familiar enough no longer to obscure its poetry, it will be found that what I have attempted to do, will be done proportionately to their measure of ability by travellers generally.—HUGH MILLER.

The earth trembles, and the waters are vexed, with the application of all those forces which science has presented for the perfection of man's dominion and power over the material world. The victory of Fulton and Fitch and Watt and Arkwright and Stephenson is complete. And should science advance into that great region of thought and speculation, where faith is to be confirmed and unerring dogmas of public economy are to be proclaimed, I am sure the last step would then have been taken toward making this great and diverse municipality as perfect in its religion and politics as it now is in all the practical affairs of active and vigorous life.

Everywhere in cultivated and civilized society may be found an intense and serious effort to infuse the accuracy of scientific investigation into all practical affairs, and into the broad foundations of the Church and the State. The scientific period has arrived. The prediction made by Dr. Young in the latter part of the last century—has been more than fulfilled.

Remembering as he did, that the last two hundred years have done much more for the promotion of knowledge than the two thousand years which preceded them, he says: 'We have, therefore, the satisfaction of viewing the knowledge of nature not only in a state of advancement, but even advancing with increasing rapidity: and the universal diffusion of a taste for science appears to promise that, as the numbers of its cultivators increases, new facts will be continually discovered, and those which are already known will be better understood and more beneficially applied.'

The history of American industry teaches that labor is not only wealth and national prosperity, but social dignity as well. Our great imperishable treasures are land and labor. Unite the two and you have the foundation upon which all the more imposing and fleeting fabrics may rest, and for the strength of which the mind of man may exhaust itself in devising means and methods. Intelligent labor, owning a well cultivated soil—this is the foundation. And around this may gather all the arts of life, in which toil shall receive a competent subsistence, and the hardships of labor may be ameliorated by that mutual understanding which should belong to an intelligent and well-educated community.—LORING.

13. *Certainty. Mr. Gladstone at Liverpool College.*—But in preparing yourselves for the combat of life, I beg you to take this also into your account, that the spirit of denial is abroad, and has challenged all religion, but especially the religion we profess, to a combat of life and death. I venture to offer you a few suggestions, in the hope that they may not be without their use. You will hear in your after-life much of the duty and delight of following free thought; and in truth the man who does not value the freedom of his thoughts deserves to be described as Homer described the slave : he is but half a man. St. Paul, I suppose, was a teacher of free thought, when he bade his converts to prove all things ; but it seems he went terribly astray when he proceeded to bid them 'hold fast that which is good.' But the free thought of which we now hear so much

seems too often to mean, thought roving and vagrant more than free, like Delos drifting on the seas of Greece without a route, a direction, or a home. Again you will hear incessantly of the advancement of the present age, and of the backwardness of those which have gone before it. And truly, it has been a wonderful age; but let us not exaggerate. It has been, and it is an age of immense mental as well as material activity: it is by no means an age abound-ing in minds of the first order, who become great, immortal teachers of mankind. It has tapped, as it were, and made disposable for man, vast natural forces; but the mental power employed, is not to be measured by the mere size of the results. To per-fect that marvel of traffic, the locomotive, has per-haps not required the expenditure of more mental strength and application and devotion than to per-fect that marvel of music, the violin. In the ma-terial sphere, the achievements of the age are plenti-ful and unmixed. In the social sphere they are great and noble, but seem ever to be confronted by a succession of new problems, which almost defy solution. In the sphere of pure intellect, I doubt whether posterity will rate us as highly as we rate ourselves. In the goods of this world we may ad-vance by strides, but it is by steps only, and not strides, and by slow, and not always steady steps, that all desirable improvement of man in the higher ranges of his being is effected. Again, my friends, you will hear much to the effect that the divisions among Christians render it impossible to say what Christianity is, and so destroy the certainty of religion. But if the divisions among Christians are remarkable, not less so is their unity in the greatest doctrines that they hold. Well nigh fifteen hundred years have passed away since the great controversies concerning the Deity and the person of the Redeemer were, after a long agony, determined. Ever since that time, amid all chance and change, more—aye, many more—than ninety-nine in every hundred Christians have with one will confessed the deity and incarnation of our Lord as the cardinal and central truths of our religion. Surely there is some comfort here—some sense of brotherhood—some glory in the past—some hope for the times that are to come.

14. *Superstition. A false divination in their sight.* —The minds of the people of England in general were, at this momentous crisis, laboring under a painful depression occasioned by the appearance of the splendid three-tailed comet, which became visible in their horizon at the commencement of the memorable year 1066, a few days before the death of King Edward. The unsettled state of the succession, and the superstitious spirit of the age, inclined all classes of persons to regard with ominous feelings of dismay and phenomenon which could be construed into a portent of evil: moreover the astrologers who foretold the approach of this comet had thought proper

to announce their prediction in an oracular distich, of which the following rude couplet is a literal translation:—

'In the year one thousand and sixty-six,
Comets to England's sons an end shall fix.'

The Norman Conquest in 1066.—The knights and archers landed first. After the soldiers came the carpenters, armorers and masons. Last of all came the duke, who stumbling as he leaped to shore, measured his majestic height upon the beach. Forthwith all raised a cry of distress. 'An evil sign is here!' exclaimed the superstitious Normans : but the duke who, in recovering himself, had filled his hands with sand cried out in a loud and cheerful voice : 'See seigneurs! I have seized England with my two hands. Without challenge no prize can be made, and that which I have grasped I will by your good help maintain.'

When William was arming for the encounter in his haste and agitation, he unwittingly put on his hawberk the hind part before. He quickly changed it, but perceiving from the looks of consternation among the by-standers, that his mistake had been observed and construed into an omen of ill, he smilingly observed : 'I have seen many a man, who, if such a thing had happened to him, would not have entered the battlefield. But I never believed in omens, nor have I ever put my faith in fortune-tellers, nor divinations of any kind, for my trust is in God.

Let not this mischance discourage you, for if this change import aught, it is that the power of my dukedom shall be turned into a kingdom.'—MISS STRICKLAND.

The king of Babylon stood at the head of the two ways, to use divination; he made his arrows bright, he consulted with images.

Astrology.—One of the most remarkable believers in that forgotten and despised science, was a late professor in the art of legerdemain. One would have thought that a person of his description ought, from his knowledge of the thousand ways in which human eyes could be deceived, to have been less than others subject to the fantasies of superstition. Perhaps the habitual use of those abstruse calculations by which in a manner surprising to the artist himself, many tricks upon cards etc., are performed, induced this gentleman to study the combination of the stars and planets with the expectation of obtaining prophetic communications. He constructed a scheme of his own nativity, calculated according to such rules of art as he could collect from the best astrological authors. The result of the past he found to be agreeable to what had hitherto befallen him, but in the important prospect of the future, a singular difficulty occurred. There were two years during the course of which he could by no means obtain any exact knowledge whether the subject of the scheme would be dead or alive. Anxious concerning so remarkable a circumstance, he gave the scheme to a brother astrologer, who was also baffled in the same manner. At one period he found the native or subject was certainly alive; at another that he was unquestionably dead; but a space of two years extended between these two terms, during which he could find no certainty as to his death or existence. The astrologer continued his exhibitions in various parts of the empire, until the period was about to expire during which his existence had been warranted as actually ascertained. At last, while he was exhibiting to a numerous audience his usual tricks of legerdemain, the hands whose activity had so often baffled the closest observer, suddenly lost their power, the cards dropped from them, and he sank down a disabled paralytic. In this state the artist languished for two years, when he was at length removed by death. The fact, if truly reported, is one of those singular coincidences which occasionally appear differing so widely from ordinary calculation, yet without which irregularities, human life would not present to mortals looking into futurity the abyss of impenetrable darkness which it is the pleasure of the Creator it should offer to them. Were everything to happen in the ordinary train of events, the future would be subject to the rules of Arithmetic, like the chances of gaming. But extraordinary events, and wonderful runs of luck defy the calculations of mankind, and throw impenetrable darkness on future contingencies.—WALTER SCOTT.

'According to our human observation it is not well
for man to know the destiny of his being in all its
details, until the trials and victories of life have
taught him, to turn such knowledge to elevating use.'

Erskine left his native land with the disheartening
prospect of dying a half-pay lieutenant:—but when
he next revisited it, he was an Ex-Chancellor, a
Peer and a Knight of the Thistle—what was far
more valuable, he had achieved for himself the reputation of the greatest forensic orator that Britain
ever produced. . . Riding over a blasted heath between Lewes and Guilford with his friend William
Adam, afterwards Lord Chief-Commissioner of the
Jury Court in Scotland, (whether from some supernatural communication, or the workings of his own
fancy I know not,) he exclaimed after a long silence :
' Willie, the time will come when I shall be invested
with the robes of the Lord Chancellor, and Star of
the Thistle will blaze on my bosom ! '—-CAMPBELL'S
CHANCELLORS.

*Why seeing times are not hidden from the Al-
mighty, do they that know him not see his days?
For man also knoweth not his time ; as the fishes that
are taken in an evil net, and as the birds that are
caught in the snare, so are the sons of men snared in
an evil time, when it falleth suddenly upon them.*

15. Men of excellent repute for wisdom, common
sense, and especially for fervid piety, have frequently
not merely entertained but courageously avowed a

lively faith in the providential and prophetic character of dreams. How far this, with the well educated, has ever deserved the respectable name of positive belief, it would require a nice and extensive investigation to determine.—TRIBUNE.

Undoubted proof has been afforded that the energy of the intellect is sometimes greater during sleep than at other times, and many a problem, it is asserted, has been solved in sleep which has puzzled the waking sense. Cabanis tells us that Franklin on several occasions mentioned to him that he had been assisted in dreams in the conduct of many affairs in which he was engaged. Condilla states that while writing his *Course of Studies* he was frequently obliged to leave the chapter incomplete and retire to bed, and that on awakening he found it, on more than one occasion, finished in his head. In like manner Condorcet would sometimes leave his complicated speculations unfinished, and after retiring to rest would find their results unfolded to him in his dreams.—HARPER'S WEEKLY.

> But though our dreams are often wild,
>   Like clouds before the driving storm,
> Yet some important may be styled,
>   Sent to admonish or inform.—NEWTON.

The same God who most expressly warns against false dreams, not unfrequently directs his people by true ones. For the sincere, who were really concerned for the truth—he discloses infallible criteria by which to distinguish genuine visions from false ones. Yet as these are modified by individual disposition they can be reduced to no objective rules.— OLSHAUSEN.

How hast thou plentifully declared the thing as it is.

Forwarned.—Some very sensible persons will acknowledge that in old times God spoke by dreams, but affirm with much boldness that he has since ceased to do so. If you ask them why? They answer, because he has now revealed his will in the Scripture, and there is no longer any need that he should instruct and admonish us by dreams. I grant that with respect to doctrines and precepts he has left us in want of nothing; but has he thereby precluded himself in any of the operations of his providence? Surely not. It is perfectly a different consideration; and the same need that there was of his interference in this way, there is still and ever must be, while man continues blind and fallible, and a creature beset with dangers which he can neither foresee nor obviate. His operations of this kind are, I allow, very rare.—COWPER.

The misery of man is great upon him. For he knoweth not that which shall be: for who can tell him when it shall be?

Lord Littleton's vision—predicting his death. The exact fulfilment.—Dr. Johnson said: 'It is the most extraordinary thing that has happened in my day. I heard it with my own ears from his uncle, Lord

Westcote. I am so glad to have every evidence of the spiritual world that I am willing to believe it.'

There is a thing that has made considerable impression on me. A week before the war at Morpeth, I dreamed distinctly many of the circumstances of our late battle off the enemy's port, and I believe I told you of it at the time; but I never dreamed that I was to be made a peer of the realm.—LORD COLLINGWOOD.

Can a devil open the eyes of the blind? Nebuchadnezzar's dream. Now thou, O Belteshazzar, declare the interpretation. All the wise men of my kingdom are not able;—but thou art able; for the spirit of the holy gods is in thee. Then Daniel was astonied for one hour and his thoughts troubled him. It is thou, O king, that art grown and become strong. They shall drive thee from men—and shall make thee to eat grass as oxen.—Wherefore, O king, let my counsel be acceptable unto thee, and break off thy sins by righteousness, and thine iniquities by showing mercy to the poor, if it may be a lengthening of thy tranquility.

17. *A certain fearful looking for of judgment.*

Henry I.—In the year 1130, the king complained to Grimbald, his Saxon physician, that he was sore disquieted of nights, and that he seemed to see a great number of husbandmen, with their rustical tools stand about him, threatening him with wrongs done against them. Sometimes he appeared to see

his knights and soldiers threatening him; which sight
so feared him in his sleep that oftimes he rose un-
drest out of his bed, took weapon in hand and
sought to kill them he could not find. Grimbald,
being a notable wise man, expounded his dreams by
true conjecture, and willed him to reform himself
by alms and prayers. . . When Henry had embarked
for England, in June 1131, he was so dismayed by
the bursting of a water-spout over the vessel and the
fury of the wind and waves, that believing that his
last hour was at hand he made a penitent acknow-
ledgment of his sins, promising to lead a new life,
if it should please God to preserve him from the
peril of death, and above all, he vowed to repeal the
oppressive impost of danegelt for seven years.

After Edward had marched through France without resistance, and, (if the truth must be spoken)
desolating as he went a bleeding and suffering country in a most ungenerous manner, his career was
stopped as he was hastening to lay seige to Paris by
the hand of God itself. One of those dreadful
thunder-storms which at distant cycles pass over the
continent of France, literally attacked the invading
army within two leagues of Chartres and wreaked
its utmost fury on the proud chivalry of England.
Six thousand of Edward's finest horses, and one
thousand of his bravest cavaliers, among whom were
the heirs of Warwick and Morley, were struck
dead before him. The guilty ambition of Edward

smote his conscience; he knelt down on the spot, and spreading his hands toward the Church of our Lady of Chartres vowed to stop the effusion of blood and make peace on the spot with France. His queen who wished well to the noble-minded king of France held him to his resolution.—MISS STRICKLAND.

And Elijah answered, If I be a man of God, then let fire come down from heaven and consume thee and thy fifty. And there came down fire from heaven and consumed him and his fifty.

And ye shall know that I am the Lord for ye have not walked in my statutes.

Charles IX.—The king thrown out into the hideous torrent of blood, became drunk with frenzy, and let slaughter have its way, till even Guise himself affected to be shocked, and interposed to put an end to it. Some twenty months later, Charles IX. lay dying of hemorrhage—he was haunted with hideous dreams; the darkness was peopled with ghosts which were mocking and mowing at him, and he would start out of his sleep to find himself in a pool of blood—blood—ever blood. The night before his end, the nurse—a Huguenot, heard him sob and sigh.

Ah! he muttered, but I was ill-advised. God have mercy on me and on my country; what will become of that? What will become of me? I am lost—I know it but too well. The nurse told him that the blood would be on the heads of those who had mis-

led him, on them and on their accursed counsels. He
sighed again and blessed God that he had left no son
to inherit his crown and his infamy.—FROUDE.

> There is no future pang,
> Can deal that justice on the self-condemned,
> He deals on his own soul.—BYRON.

19. *Conscience.*—*Beyond measure I persecuted the
Church of God, and wasted it.*—*I verily thought with
myself, that I sought to do many things contrary to
the name of Jesus.*

Who sees not that our judgments of virtue and
vice, right and wrong, are not always formed from
an enlightened and dispassionate use of our reason
in the investigation of truth ? They are more generally formed from the nature of the religion we
profess; from the quality of the civil government
under which we live; from the general manners of
the age, or the particular manners of the persons
with whom we associate; from the books we have
read at a more advanced period; and from other
accidental causes.—WATSON.

Now one of the most curious, entertaining, and
instructive things on earth is the observation of the
various lights in which a pictorial work that touches
the springs of social action is regarded by the different thinkers, writers, and talkers, who represent
classes. In seriously answering the inquiry: 'What
does all this amount to ?' how queerly opposed to
each other are the summings up which express the

main lesson of ideal or of practical value.—ART CRI-
TIC.

*And when they saw him they worshipped him, but
some doubted.*

*And when they heard of the resurrection from the
dead, some mocked and others said: We will hear
thee again of this matter.*

The confiscation of Church property was an enormous loss of Church power. It held two-thirds of
this city in possession. It held mortgages in as large
a portion of the country. Letting its money at a
low figure and on liberal and long terms, it gradually
became an enormous savings bank, and controlled
the whole landed interest of the country. Its con-
vents covered hundreds of acres in the heart of the
city, and were adorned in the highest degree that
art and wealth could devise. Gardens, lakes, marble
cloisters, elegantly wrought in polished marble,
churches of splendor in construction and ornamenta-
tion, were the unseen luxurious abodes of the world-
denying friars and nuns. Corruption of the most
startling sort abounded; and money, the sinews of
the state, was in the hands exclusively of the corrupted and corruptors. Good men may have been
involved in this arrangement, may have presided over
it. Good men have been connected with every controlling evil the world has ever seen. An orthodox
Congregational minister called his burning satire
against New England's demoralization under rum

'Deacon Giles' Distillery,' and the slaveholding system of English West Indies was supported by rectors
of the Episcopal Church, and of our own land by
bishops of the Methodist Church, South. So we are
all in condemnation and none can throw stones at the
former growth of the Roman Church in Mexico.—
G. HAVEN.

20. *What is truth?—*

What a loud roaring loose and empty matter is
this tornado of vociferation men call 'Public Opinion,' tragically howling round a man who has to
stand silent the while; and scan wisely under pain
of death, the altogether inarticulate, dumb, and inex-
orable matter which the gods call Fact.—CARLYLE.

Have faith in truth, never in numbers. The great
surge of numbers rolls up noisily and imposingly,
but flats out on the shore, and slides back into the
muds of oblivion. But the true opinion is the ocean
itself, calm in its rest, eternal in its power. Its life
is in moral ideas, which is the life of God.—BEECHER.

The law of truth is in his mouth.—

Think truly and thy thoughts
Shall the world's famine feed;
Speak truly, and each word of thine
Shall be a fruitful seed.
Live truly, and thy life shall be
A great and noble creed.—BONAR.

7*

Prove thou the rejected stone,
　True to the Eternal Square;
And the mighty Builder may
　In the wondrous scheme of man
Set thy life some glorious day,
　The grand Key-Stone of his plan.
　　　　　　　—E. A. BROWNE.

A soul at one with what is just,
　And balanced like a poised lance·
A will to quit the narrow lea,
　Whose stilly bounds the winds forsake.
　　　　　　　—WILLARD.

The one great effort of such a mind is to divest itself of all prejudice, of all desire that may operate in the secret chambers of· the mind and derange the logical processes and vitiate the results to be obtained. The mind having adopted this method, pursues its inductive and deductive processes with a supreme desire for the truth, whether the truth be agreeable or disagreeable. This quality of mind is not simply an intellectual virtue; it is a moral one as well. We may look with confidence to such a mind for the supreme desire of justice, not only to truth for its own sake, but for justice to individuals for truth's sake. Blind, contagious, intellectual impulse finds no lodgment in such a mind.—PATTERSON.

Of literary merit Johnson, as we all know, was a sagacious, but a most severe judge. Such was his discernment that he pierced into the most secret springs of human actions : and such was his integrity that he always weighed the moral characters of his fellow-creatures in the ' balance of the sanctuary.' He was too courageous to propitiate a rival, and too proud to truckle to a superior. By the testimony of such a man, impertinence must be abashed and malignity itself softened.—MACAULAY.

21. *Israel's choice. Give us a king. Samuel prayed. The Lord said hearken to their voice yet protest solemnly. They have not rejected thee, but they have rejected me that I should not reign over them.*

A poor prophet in a mantle, though conversant with the visions of the Almighty, looked mean in their eyes who judged by outward appearance ; but a king in a purple robe, with his guard and officers of state would look great. When God chose a king after his own heart, he pitched upon one who was not at all remarkable for the height of his stature, or anything in his countenance, but the innocency and sweetness that appeared there. But when he chose a king after the people's heart, who aimed at nothing so much as stateliness and grandeur, he pitched upon this huge, tall man, who if he had no other good qualities would look great.—HENRY.

Countess—. . . . Is this the scourge of France,
    Is this the Talbot so much feared abroad,
    That with his name, the mothers still their babes ?
    I see, report is fabulous and false :

I thought I should have seen some Hercules,
A second Hector for his grim aspect
And large proportion of his strong-knit limbs.
Alas! this is a child, a silly dwarf:
It cannot be, this weak and writhled shrimp
Should strike such terror to his enemies.
Tal.—Madam, I have been bold to trouble you
But, since your ladyship is not at leisure,
I'll sort some other time to visit you.
        (*The gates being forced, enter soldiers.*)
Countess—Victorious Talbot! pardon my abuse:
I find thou art no less than fame hath bruited,
And more than may be gathered by thy shape.
Let my presumption not provoke thy wrath;
For I am sorry that with reverence
I did not entertain thee as thou art.
Tal.—Be not dismay'd, fair lady; nor misconstrue
The mind of Talbot, as you did mistake
The outward composition of his body.
What you have done hath not offended me.
               —KING HENRY IV.

The bee that gathers treasures from every flower
has not the finest coating. The eagle that soars on
majestic wing to the birth of the morning has not
the most glittering plumage. It is the butterfly that
idly floats on the passing breeze that the fopling
emulates.—DEHON.

Irregularity of feature is the rule. They are
often even distorted: and yet I must say that I have
seen some magnificent countenances and figures
among the German peasantry. Here for instance is
one—an old woman—she must be at least sixty.

She stops for a moment, and leans upon her spade, while the youngster who drops potatoes for her, likely enough her grandchild, runs off to get her basket filled from a supply that a girl had just brought up. And as the old dame, I was going to say, though she is a poor, old peasant woman, turns about and looks up for a minute, the old rag that she has bound around her head falls back, revealing a profile, a forehead that would have graced a court. The gray locks that float in the light breeze were surely thick and flowing two-score of years ago. The cheeks, the bare neck, and thinly covered shoulders, wrinkled and sunken with years of toil and care, have lost their charms: but traces of lines of delicate beauty and stately grace linger even yet. And now, as she turns toward me, she meets my gaze with an unabashed, courteous, and even dignified look; and then there is a slight play of the features, a glance at the spade, at the toil worn hands, and back to me again, with her rich, black eyes looking straight in mine, and I think: 'Fortunate is it for your peace of mind, young man, that that old woman isn't forty years younger.' There is, to the glory of the human soul be it said, a germ of pride therein, that the meanest poverty cannot root out, and often one is met even in the lowest walks of life by those whose very air and mien proclaim: ' Even in my rags and misery I am your equal.'—TRIBUNE COR.

> . . . He has, I know not what,
> Of greatness in his looks, and of high fate,
> That almost awes me.—DRYDEN.

'The glare of outward beauty is soon darkened, but there is a beauty foreshadowing itself in the grace of action and feeling which the more the mind is used to, the more it chooses to rest on it.'

'It is said the spirit's beauty cannot be shut within as you would shut the diamond in its casket, hiding all its light; but that the radiance illuminating the inner temple will spread itself over the face proclaiming to all who come near 'here dwells an angel.'

A wicked heart—covered with silver dross.

> . . . Your thief looks in the crowd,
> Exactly like the rest, or rather better;
> 'Tis only at the bar, or in the dungeon,
> That wise men know your felon by his features.—BYRON.

22. *Types.*—She to higher hopes
   Was destined, in a finer mould was wrought,
   And tempered with a purer, brighter flame.—AKENSIDE.

The dove is universally allowed to be one of the most beautiful objects in nature. The brilliancy of her plumage, the splendor of her eye, the innocence of her look, the excellence of her disposition, and the purity of her manners have been the theme of admiration in every age. To the snowy whiteness of her wings, and the rich golden hues that adorn her neck, the inspired Psalmist alludes in most elegant strains. She is the chosen emblem of simplicity, gentleness, chastity, and feminine timidity, and for this reason, as well as for their abounding in the East, they were chosen as offerings to Jehovah.'

. . . *the wings of a dove covered with silver, and her feathers with yellow gold.*

The Rose.—' In native white and red,
    The rose and lily stand,
    And free from pride their beauties spread,
    To show thy skillful hand.'

True, you were not made to be a great, coarse sun-flower, nor a full Provence-rose, but to be a beautiful, little Scotch rose—to show the world that God could plant such beautiful flowers on the bleak mountains and in the misty valleys of Scotland—a great rose condensed into a miniature one—as if to show how much that is beautiful can be put into a very small space. Again, you complain of the heat of noon,—the very time when the strong light is falling on you, and painting your face with colors which nothing but the noon-day sun could possibly bestow. If you want your glorious colors, you must have the hot pencil of the sun paint them.—TODD.

    Thy emblem, gracious queen, the British rose,
    Type of sweet rule and gentle majesty.—PRIOR.

Hannah More.—There was an air of graceful, un-affected ease : an instinctive regard to the most deli-cate proprieties of social intercourse ; a readiness to communicate ; and yet a desire to lessen the dignity

of conscious merit, united with the humility of the
devoted Christian : in short there was such an assemblage of intellectual and moral excellences beaming
forth in every expresssion, and look, and attitude,
that I could scarcely conceive of a more perfect ex-
hibition of human character.

23. Everywhere womanhood is standing up our
equal.   We are finding out by slow degrees the old
law of God ; we are getting back to the old truths of
childhood.   As of old in Eden manhood and womanhood are being wed anew—wed in dignified equality
as high help-meets in the work of the world.—Ec-
LECTIC.

He fashioneth their hearts alike.—
Look to God for that divine, celestial welding that
shall make you goldenly one.   The perfect ideal love
and heart union, is that which takes place, when two
minds are bound together that have respectively the
capacity to give to the whole of each other's mind
appropriate stimulus and gratification.—BEECHER.

' The attraction which is the basis of this union is
of a compound character, connecting with it some of
the highest and most ennobling virtues of which
human nature is capable.'

Mrs. E. Judson.—His discerning eye saw the slumbering traits of noble missionary character, while her
delicate and beautiful genius ran through a larger
compass of correspondences to his versatile and
many-sided nature, than that of either of her prede-

cessors. Ann Hasseltine more than met all the demand of his earlier years of youthful and heroic action. Sarah Boardman shed the light of one of the most exquisite of womanly natures over the calmer scenes of his manhood. Emily, with a heroism not less devoted, with a womanliness not less pure and gentle, met his ripe culture, his keen intellectuality, his imaginative and poetic temperament, with a richness and variety of endowments which belonged to neither of these admirable women.—KENDRICK.

The fervid, burning eloquence, the deep pathos, the touching tenderness, the elevation of thought, the intense beauty of expression which characterized these private teachings were not only beyond what I had ever heard before, but such as I feel sure surprized himself.—E. JUDSON.

The Old.—The higher the civilization, the more nearly is companionship of the sexes reached. The highest civilization is yet to come, and with it such companionship in its completeness we may first look for it here; for though we are the newest of nations, we have done more than any other to discard old and pernicious traditions. The land of chivalry, in a truer and better sense than the knights-errant were capable of understanding, has long been in this republic, though our future is doomed to shame our present, and excite emulation elsewhere.

The German, who is our remote ancestor, has no pleasures from which women are shut out, and he is one of the most domestic, honest, and composed of mortals. Lineage moves in cycles; we are going back by degrees to the customs of our progenitors. We see the influence of Teutonic habits upon our own people already, and we take kindly to the examples of our own race.

We Americans require the social element in our diversions, which are very melancholy in the main. We need enjoyment, instead of excitement, solace instead of selfishness, comfort instead of intensity.

We want quiet talk (or pleasant silence), careless repose, the assurance of sympathy, gentle stimulants: not boisterous speech, impertinent egotism, restless repression, coarse stories, vulgar profanity, and fiery potations.

Before the present century has passed, our dissipations will be restored, I predict, to the significance of recreations. Women will be our partners in them, and they will bring new tastes, new desires, new atmospheres, and by their wholesome presence and exquisite tact will transform us into finer creatures than have been reflected even from the mirror of our vanity. Companionship will have rendered the sexes just, conscientious, truthful to each other; will have taken flippant flattery from the lip and put cordial appreciation in the mind; will have substituted voices for echoes. purposes for words, aspirations for assumptions. Companionship will have served as instruction, reason, and intuition.—BROWNE.

Buckle.—The influence of his mother led him to value the mental sympathy and companionship of women. He had a keen appreciation of what their peculiar intellectual quality should do for society. His extreme gentleness combined with power made him a favorite.—TRIBUNE.

Womanly women are very kindly critics, except to themselves, and now and then to their own sex. The less there is of sex about a woman the more she is to be dreaded. But take a real woman at her best moment—well dressed enough to be pleased with herself, not so resplendent as to be a show and a sensation, with the varied outside influences that set vibrating the harmonic notes of her nature stirring in the air about her—and what has social life to compare with one of those vital interchanges of thought and feeling with her that makes an hour memorable ? What can equal her tact, her delicacy, her subtlety of apprehension, her quickness to feel the changes of temperature as the warm and cool currents of thought blow by turns ? At one moment she is microscopically intellectual, critical, scrupulous in judgment as an analyst's balance : and in the next as sympathetic as the open rose, that sweetens the wind from whatever quarter it finds its way to her bosom. It is in the hospitable soul of a woman that a man forgets he is a stranger, and so becomes natural and truthful, at the same time that he is mesmerized by all those divine differences which make her a mystery and bewilderment.—HOLMES

'Her fair soul like scent of flowers unseen
Sweetens the turmoil of long centuries.'

The truly great are always good. You used to say that *talents were always* formidable. I think not so. Superior beings are necessarily benignant; they guide us and guard us, not like the jostling of a mob, but by a guiding, invisible influence. I never fear a great man, I only fear and hate what the slang of the world calls a *clever* man; that is, generally, a pert, half-wise man. In the other sex the women who bear sway over the generality of minds, are called accomplished and beautiful women; they are like those half-wise men, generally thought formidable: they are to me very great objects of terror, just as self-conceit and bad dispositions are terrible! But let me see the woman who is truly admirable, and I fancy the most shy and ungainly admirer of female excellence, like myself, will be very much at his ease and destitute of all fear and diffidence in her presence. The truly beautiful, the truly wise, the truly good do not abash the most retiring. The friendship of wise men—the sentiments with which I have regarded my real heroines convince me of this.— THOMAS CAMBPELL.

She comprehended for the first time, how sweet a thing it is to develop, reveal, express one's self in the presence of a great soul that measures with an appreciating, admiring and loving eye, every utterance and every power.—HOLLAND.

'Great natures are never injured by appreciation and preference: even when frankly and openly expressed. On the contrary, they are encouraged by it and grow nobler: nor do they ever misunderstand it. It is only the petty, inferior mind which puts a wrong construction on such regard, and wounds us by its vanity and self-conceit.'

> . . . Modest doubt is called
> The beacon of the wise.—SHAKESPEARE.

26. That renowned champion, Sir Bertrand Du Guesclin, was one of the prisoners at Poictiers. One day, when Queen Philippa was entertaining at her court a number of the noble French prisoners, the prince of Wales proposed that Du Guesclin should name his own ransom, according to the etiquette of the times, adding that whatever sum he mentioned, be it small or great, should set him free. The valiant Breton valued himself at one hundred thousand crowns; the prince of Wales started at the immense sum and asked Sir Bertrand how he could ever expect to raise such an enormous ransom? 'I know,' replied the hero, 'a hundred knights in my native Bretagne who would mortgage their last acre rather than Du Guesclin should either lanquish in prison, or be rated below his value. Yea, and there is not a woman in France now toiling at her distaff who would not devote a year's earnings to set me free, for well have I deserved of their sex. And if all the

fair spinners of France employ their hands to redeem me, think you, prince, whether I shall bide much longer with you?' Queen Philippa, who had listened with great attention to the discussion, now spoke. 'I name,' she said, 'fifty thousand crowns, my son, as my contribution toward your gallant prisoner's ransom: for though an enemy to my husband, a knight who is famed for the courteous attention he has afforded to my sex deserves the assistance of every woman.'—MISS STRICKLAND.

'Give us a man, young or old, high or low, on whom we know that we can thoroughly depend, who will stand firm when others fail, the friend faithful and true, the adviser honest and fearless, the adversary just and chivalrous; in such an one there is a fragment of the Rock of Ages,—a sign that there has been a prophet among us.'

If you are so favored as to have a friend worthy the name, whose eye brightens and whose heart replenishes yours, in whose nature you find the complement and touch the equilibrium of your own, that is a very different affair.—ALGER.

I am arrived at last in the presence of a man so real and equal that I may drop even those undermost garments of dissimulation, courtesy, and second-thought which men never put off, and may deal with him with the simplicity and wholeness with which one chemical atom meets another.—EMERSON.

Great souls know each other. Years are the servitors of slower natures, and nurse men into mutual confidences. There are certain touches that fine natures know instantly conclusive of all the rest—the free-masonry of the sons of God.—BEECHER.

For let the swaying, surging hosts throughout the valley deliver themselves as they can from the confusion of tongues, the wanderers among the mountains ought to understand the signals they see flaring from crag and gorge and pinnacle.—ATLANTIC MONTHLY.

'Thy sunlike soul my weary way hath lighted,
Speaking in silence through thy life to mine.—BURLEIGH

27. If your friend has displeased you, you shall not sit down to consider it, for he has already lost all memory of the passage, and has doubled his power to serve you, and ere you can rise up again will burden you with blessings.—EMERSON.

And to be wroth with one we love
Doth work like madness in the brain.—COLERIDGE.

Every man's experience must teach him that quarrels between friends are best healed when they are healed most promptly. The alienation which was at first a pain, becomes by time habitual ; and the mantle of charity being withdrawn, the faults of each become more and more distinct to the other, and thus the bitterest hates spring from the ashes of the closest friendship.—DAVIS.

Charles Dickens relates this touching story of Douglas Jerrold. Of his generosity, I had a proof within these two or three years which it saddens me to think of now. There had been estrangement between us—not involving angry words, and a good many months had passed without my ever seeing him in the streets; when it fell out that we dined each with his own separate party in the stranger's room of the club. Our chairs were almost back to back, and I took mine after he was seated, and at dinner (I am sorry to remember), and· did not look that way. Before we had sat long, he openly wheeled his chair round, stretched out both hands in an engaging manner, and said aloud with a bright and loving face that I can see as I write to you: ' Let us be friends again. A life is not long enough for this.'

' A more glorious victory cannot be gained over a man, than when an injury begins on his part, kindness should begin on ours.'

How long must the sinner call upon God before he sees the smile of Love making bright the heavens, glad the earth, possible all blessing? For he hath built no walls, fastened no bars, blasted no present, cursed no future.

If love be large, rich, free, strong enough, it brings itself with one bound into the heavenly kingdom, where the Powers of Darkness had well nigh prevailed.—ATLANTIC MONTHLY.

28. *What is my beloved more than another?*

Your friend, who shall describe him, or worthily paint what he is to you? No merchant or lawyer,

nor farmer nor statesman claims your suffrage, but a
kingly soul.　He comes to you from God—a prophet,
a seer, a revealer.　He has a clear vision.　His love
is reverence.　He goes into the penetralia of your
life, not presumptuously, but with uncovered head,
unsandalled feet ; and pours libations at the inner-
most shrine.　His incense is grateful.　A golden
glow suffuses your atmosphere.　A vague, fine cc-
stasy thrills to the sources of life, and earth lays
hold on heaven.　Such friend;hip is worship.　You
only know that your whole being bows with humility
and utter thankfulness to him who thus crowns you
monarch of all realms.

You go back into your solitudes : all is silent as
aforetime, but you cannot forget that a voice once
resounded there.—GAIL HAMILTON.

> ' As one entranced will sometimes gaze afar
>   Into the deep blue night,
> At the sweet radiance of some special star
>   That shines supremely bright;
> His look concentred—all the rest unrecked,
>   Their glowing courses run ;
> Though by ten myriad gems the heavens are decked,
>   To him there is but one.
>
> So I look up into a glorious face,
>   Into a calm, kind eye,
> Radiant with queenly nobleness an　grace—
>   Clear as a cloudless sky.
> Not bright as brooks that o'er the shallows roll,
>   But oh, so pure and deep,

8

With fathomless serenity of soul,
  Like ocean in a sleep!

There might be faces fifty times as fair,
  Oh, dear loved lady mine!
But though there were, I'd neither know nor care;
  I'm blind to all but thine.'

'There is, there has ever been but one voice for me. For answer the organist lifted the lid of the artist's piano, touched a few notes and sang. Was that the voice that once brought out the applause of the people rushing and roaring like the waves of the sea? The same etherealized, strengthened, meeting the desire of the trained and cultured man, as once it had the impassioned aspiration of youth. He stood there as of old completely subject to her will; and of old she had worked for good, as one of God's accredited angels. Every evil passion in those days had stood rebuked before the charmed circle ot her influences: a voice to long for as the hart longs for the waterbrooks; a spirit to trust for work, or for love, or for truth,—'truest truth' and stanchest loyalty, as one might trust those who are delivered forever from the power of temptation.—The eyes so large and blue: the lips with their story of firm courage and true genius, so grand in calm. A figure however not likely to attract the many, but whom it held for once it held forever.—ATLANTIC MONTHLY.

30. Leave to the diamond its ages to grow, nor expect to accelerate the births of the eternal. He

only is fit for this society who is magnanimous, who is sure that greatness and goodness are always economy; who is not swift to intermeddle with his fortunes. Reverence is a great part of it. Treat your friend as a spectacle. Let us buy our entrance to this guild by a long probation: Respect so far the holy laws of this fellowship, as not to prejudice its perfect flower by your impatience for its opening. We must be our own before we can be another's. The least defect of self-possession vitiates the entire relation. There can never be deep peace between you, never mutual respect, until in their duality, each stands for the entire world.—EMERSON.

> Wait, and Love himself will bring
> The drooping flower of knowledge
> Changed to fruit of wisdom.
> Wait, my faith is large in time,
> And that which shapes it to some perfect end.
> —TENNYSON.

I am not sure that the ladies understand the full value of the influence of absence. Distance, in truth, produces in idea the same effect as in real perspective. Objects are softened and rounded, and rendered doubly graceful; the harsher and more ordinary points of character are mellowed down, and those by which it is remembered are the more striking outlines that mark sublimity, grace or beauty. There are mists to dim the mental as well as the natural horizon, to conceal what is less pleasing in distant objects: and there are happy lights to stream in full glory upon those points which can profit by brilliant illumination.—WALTER SCOTT.

The hues of the opal, the light of the diamond, are not to be seen if the eye is too near. Let us carry it with what grandeur of spirit we can. —EMERSON.

'And still my fancy paints you near,
    Though all the room is lone and bare,
And off at eventide I hear
    Your phantom footstep on the stair.

A presence in the gathering gloom,
    Thrills all my pulses with delight,
And seems to glorify the room,
    With loveliness denied my sight.

Friendship. —A ruddy drop of manly blood
        The surging sea outweighs;
    The world uncertain comes and goes,
        The rooted lover stays.

I fancied he was fled,
    And after many a year,
Glowed unexhausted kindliness,
    Like daily sunrise there.

My careful heart was free again,
    O friend, my bosom said,
Through thee alone the sky is arched,
    Through thee the rose is red.

All things through thee take nobler form
    And look beyond the earth:
The mill-round of our fate appears
    A sun-path in thy worth.

Me too thy nobleness hath blessed
 . To master my despair,
The fountains of thy sudden life,
 Are through thy friendship fair.—EMERSON.

If the eternal ray, that heavenly was,
To no false earthly fire be reconciled,
The drop shall mingle with its native main,
The ray shall meet its kindred ray again.
 —MRS. HEMANS.

Oh! in that future let us think
 To hold each heart the heart that shares,
With them the immortal waters drink,
 And, soul in soul, grow deathless theirs.—BYRON.

2. *September*—Oh fairest month of all the year!
 Oh, sweetest days in life! they meet
Within, without, is autumn clear,
September here, September there,
 So tranquil and so sweet!

Oft have I watched all night with grief,
 All night with joy, and which is best?
Ah, both were sharp, and both were brief,
My heart was like a wind-blown leaf;
 I give them both for rest.—SPENCER.

The sultry summer past, September comes,
Soft twilight of the slow declining year,
More sober than the buxom, blooming May,
And therefore less the favorite of the world;
But dearest month of all to pensive minds.—WILCOX.

September! There are thoughts in thy heart of
death. Thou art doing a secret work, and heaping
up treasures for another year. The unborn infant-

buds which thou art tending are more than all the living leaves. Thy robes are luxuriant, but worn with softened pride. More dear, less beautiful than June, thou art the heart's mouth. Thy hands are stretched out, and clasp the glowing palm of August, and the fruit-sending hand of October. Thou dividest them asunder, and art thyself molded of them both.—BEECHER.

> ' Thou hast a token in the sky,
>   A music in thy wandering winds,
> A strength in thy maturity
>   In which the soul a solace finds.'

3. Happiness consists in the multiplicity of agreeable consciousness. There is nothing, Sir, too little for so little a creature as man. It is by studying little things that we attain the great art of having as little misery and as much happiness as possible. Pound St. Paul's church into atoms and consider any single atom; it is to be sure, good for nothing: but put all these atoms together and you have St Paul's church.—JOHNSON.

Miss Sedgewick writes of the poor peasantry of Europe that ' a very little suffices to make them happy. A thoughtful, serious view of past, present and future is not theirs.'

' Men should be intelligent and earnest. They must also make us feel that they have a controlling, happy future opening before them, whose early twilights already kindle in the passing hour.'

4. *Refinement.*—The effect of a frame or stone house is immense on the tranquility, power and refinement of the builder. A man in a cave, or in a camp, a nomad will die with no more of an estate than the wolf or the horse leaves. But so simple a labor as a house being achieved, his chief enemies are kept at bay. He is safe from the teeth of wild animals, from frost, sun-stroke and weather; and fine faculties begin to yield their fine harvest. Invention and art are born; manners, and social beauty, and delight. —EMERSON.

> . . . Spirits are not finely
> Touched but to fine issues.—SHAKESPEARE.

> *Wealth.*—' My mind to me a kingdom is.'

The pleasure of thought to a well-directed mind, the pleasure of sensible communion with the higher world, and even the delectations of a chastened imagination, have in reality more and stronger attractions, than anything to be afforded by caterers to voluptuousness. Will not this reality yet open upon the human mind, to turn it away from the outward, however gorgeous, magnificent, and seductive? —CHURCH.

6. *Your brethren that hated you, that cast you out for my name's sake said, Let the Lord be glorified.*

The severest part of self-denial consists in encountering the disapprobation, the envy, the hatred of one's dearest friends. All who enter the straight and narrow path in good earnest, soon find themselves in a climate extremely uncongenial to the growth of pride.—JUDSON.

Cast thy heart firmly upon the Lord, and fear not the judgment of man, when conscience testifieth of thy dutifulness and innocency. They that to-day take thy part, to-morrow may be against thee, and often do they turn right round like the wind. Put all thy trust in God; let Him be thy fear; he shall answer for thee and will do in all things what is best for thee.

7. I have also holy books for my comfort and for the glass of my life.—KEMPIS.

> ' My life, this lovely human life,
> Has more than purple splendor,
> And kingly guests come day by day,
> Their kingly gifts to render.'

' The scholar only knows how dear these silent yet eloquent companions of pure thoughts and innocent hours become in the season of adversity. When all that is worldly turns to dross around us, these retain their steady value. When friends grow cold and the converse of intimates languishes into vapid civility and common place, these only continue the unaltered countenance of happier days and cheer us with that true friendship which never deceived hope nor deserted sorrow.'

Athens.—Who shall say how many thousands have been made wiser, happier, and better by those pursuits in which she has taught mankind to engage; to how many the studies which took their rise from her have been wealth in poverty—liberty in bondage, —health in sickness,—society in solitude. Her power is indeed manifested in the bar, in the senate, in the field of battle, in the schools of philosophy. But these are not her glory. Wherever literature consoles sorrow, or assuages pain,—wherever it brings gladness to eyes which fail with wakefulness and tears and ache for the dark house and the long sleep, —there is exhibited in its noblest form the immortal influence of Athens.—MACAULAY.

9. *The wild beasts of the desert shall also meet with the wild beasts of the island, and the satyr shall.cry to his fellow, the screech owl also shall rest there; and find for herself a place of rest. There shall the great owl make her nest, and lay, and hatch, and gather under her shadow. There shall the vultures also be gathered, every one with her mate. Seek ye out of the book of the Lord and read, no one of these shall fail, of none shall want her mate.*

Lone flower that blooms amid the wild,
To breathe thy fragrance and to die,
Even unknown by mortal eye,
    Sweet prairie child!

Lone star that spangles midnight pall,
Lone bird that in the woodland sings,
Lone rill that from the rock-vein springs,
    God sees ye all!

Lone soul that toils in earth's great wild,
To weep and sigh and thus depart,

8*

> Uncared for by one human heart—
>> Truth's martyr child !.
>
> Thy tears are dew drops God doth kiss,
> Thy sighs are perfumes angels breathe
> From garland's woven by love that wreathe
>> The saints in bliss.—BULKLEY.

What human heart has ever found a sympathy that satisfied it either in Nature or in man? After all these afford, there remains a deep and painful craving that pleads, from time to time, for a sympathy that is higher, richer, and more complete. The more there is of culture and refinement, and especially the more of the finer endowments of genius, the intenser this conscious want. It is in truth the godlike going out after the Divine and Infinite, to which it is allied : and if by unbelief the soul be rendered incapable of finding this, the result is inward restlessness, and sometimes a deep and habitual wretchedness. One cannot read the writings of such a man as Shelley, for example, without constantly perceiving that with all his wealth of intellect and imagination, and his exquisite perceptions of the beautiful, his heart was tortured by longings for sympathetic responses which he utterly failed to find in human society, in the natural world, or in his own ideals. But let one who has sought elsewhere for sympathy and has not found it, at last find God and come into a conscious fellowship with him, and the case is altogether different. To the reality and the tenderness of God's sympathy with those that love him, the entire Scriptures, and the best Christian experience alike bear testimony. By Christ in whom dwelleth all the fulness of the Godhead bodily, the sympathy of mutual love, and personal living contact and communion is positively pledged as the grand encouragement of faithful disciples. It has never disappointed. More intimate and complete than any sympathy with creatures, it has proved immeasurably rich and sweet, it is a commingling of the divine and the human affections to which no parallel exists. The inexpressible desires which Nature and man leave yearning still find in it all of love, and tenderness and spiritual intercommunication that are required to fill them perfectly. Our communion is with the Father and His son Jesus Christ.—PALMER.

A trembling feeling of a Presence comes upon me at times which makes inward solitariness a trifle to talk about.—ROBERTSON.

> 'My Saviour, come abide with me to-night,
> My only Guest!
> My loneliness to thee, I need not tell,
> O, give me rest!'

How shall I bring thee into my house, I that have so often offended thy most benign countenance? What meaneth this so gracious condescension? Lord, how often shall I resign myself and wherein shall I forsake myself?

Always, and every hour; as well in small things

as in great. I except nothing. Otherwise, how cans't thou be mine and I thine unless thou be stripped of all self-will and with entire simplicity follow Jesus only. Then shall all vain imaginations, evil perturbations and superfluous cares fly away.—KEMPIS.

' Wesley's experience, nurtured by habitual prayer and deepened by unwearied exertion in the cause of the Saviour, deepened into that steadfast faith and solid peace which the grace of God perfected in him to the close of his long and active life.'

A Christian should possess such quietness and dignity of spirit, that resting in the consciousness of God's love and approval, he will not be greatly moved by the applause or displeasure of his fellows.— BEECHER.

Leavitt.—He knew how to combine dignity with meekness, cheerfulness with submission, how to retain that personality which was the essence of his power ; how to nourish his soul with ideas, rather than to starve it with memories and regrets ; how to identify himself with God's purposes, and thus to live above the world ; and, most of all, how in the largeness and the wealth of his own nature to separate himself from mean men, so that, however their meannesses or detractions might accost the eye or the ear, they could not intrude within the sphere of his consciousness, so as to disturb his peace.—THOMPSON.

One must remember that nothing can, without his

consent, interpose between him and his soul's communion and life, that circumstances cannot take away the Supreme presence.—MILLS.

10. *And he was transfigured before them.*

> 'If ever on the Mount with thee,
> I seem to soar in vision bright,
> With thoughts of coming agony,
> Stay thou the too presumptuous flight.

Can ye drink of the cup that I drink of?

Archbishop Leighton.—He reckoned the greater number of the regular clergy in Roman Catholic countries to be little better than—rapacious drones; at the same time that he recognized among them a few specimens of extraordinary growth in religion; and thought he had discovered in the piety of some conventual recluses, a peculiar and celestial flavor which could hardly be met with elsewhere. Of their sublime devotion he often spoke with an admiration approaching to rapture: and much he wished that the sons of a purer faith and discipline could match them in that seraphic strength and swiftness of wing, by which they soared to the topmost branches of divine contemplation, and cropped the choicest clusters of celestial fruitage. Would Christians retreat occasionally from the busy whirl and tumult of life, and give themselves time to think, they would become enamored of those beauties which lie above the natural ken on the summit of God's holy mountain!— LEIGHTON'S BIOGRAPHER.

Heaven.   God shall redeem my soul from the power of the grave, for he shall receive me.

O most blessed mansion of the city which is above! O most clear day of eternity which night obscureth not, but the highest truth ever enlighteneth!   O day ever joyful, ever secure, and never changing into a contrary state.   To the saints it shineth glowing with everlasting brightness, but to those that are pilgrims on the earth, it appeareth only afar off as it were through a glass darkly.—KEMPIS.

Thine eyes shall see the King in his beauty, and thou shall behold the land that is afar off.

> As the bird to its sheltering nest,
>   When the storm on the hills is abroad,
> So her spirit hath flown from this world of unrest,
>   To repose on the bosom of God.—BURLEIGH.

And to her was granted that she should be arrayed in fine linen, clean and white, for the fine linen is the righteousness of saints.

Does life appear miserable that gives thee opportunities of earning such a reward?   Is death to be feared, that will carry thee to so happy an existence?   Think not man was made in vain, who has such an eternity reserved for him.—SPECTATOR.

> ‘The hour, the hour, the parting hour,
>   That takes from this dark world the power,
>   And lays at once the thorn and flower
>   On the same withering bier, my soul!

The hour that ends all earthly woes,
And gives the wearied soul repose :
How soft, how sweet, that last long close
    Of mortal hope and fear, my soul !

To feel we only sleep to rise
In sunnier lands and fairer skies ;
To bind again our broken ties
    In ever living love, my soul.'

Who shall dwell in thy holy hill ? He that walketh uprightly, and worketh righteousness, and speaketh the truth in his heart.

    ' Whose soul no vanity allures ! '

The capacity of being blessed in heaven resides in a character that is capable of receiving happiness through spiritual causations.—BEECHER.

Because I live ye shall live also.

Christ, his life, his love, his principles, must be looked at with a steadier gaze, so that there may be a continued transformation into his likeness. Little habits of evil must be daily corrected,—for only by this culture of spiritual strength can the soul become strong enough to do battle with its mightier foes : —the last cloud passing away, the last stain washed out from the garments of the soul ; only when we come into the presence of Him who is light itself.— BEECHER.

    Dwell thou with him, keeping thy garments clean
      From earthly stain—thus living to his praise,
    Thou on some signal day with raptured vision /

Shall glide into the bliss of life elysian
And see thy God.—LINTHAL.

These are they who shall stand by the great white throne, who shall adorn the temple not made with hands, whose builder is God.

14. I doubt if S. is not too innocent to become sublimely excellent; her heart is purity and kindness, her recollections are complacent, her wishes and intentions are all good. In such a mind conscience becomes effeminate for want of hard exercise. She is exempted from those revulsions of the heart; that remorse, those self-indignant regrets, those impetuous convictions, which sometimes assist to scourge the mind away from its stationary habits into such region of daring and arduous virtue as it would never have reached, nor even thought of, but for this mighty impulse of pain. Witness Albany in Cecilia. Vehement emotion, mortifying contrast, shuddering alarm sting the mind into an exertion of power it was unconscious of before and urge it on with restless velocity toward the attainment of that moral eminence short of which it would equally scorn and dread to repose. We fly from pain or terror more eagerly than we pursue good; yet both these causes aid our advance.—FOSTER.

I think of what *thy* life hath been—
So pure and sweet though not serene—
So toned by grief, that gently fell
Like moonlight in a slumbering dell,

Or far-off sound of chapel-bell,
Faintly afloat through forests dim,
Or tremulous waves of vesper hymn.

*   *   *   *   *

I think of what *my* life hath been—
So small of good, so large of sin—
So like a shore where ocean beats
Forever, and the osprey greets
The ghost-like mists with ghostly screams;
Where angry tempests' lightning-gleams
Much frequenter than sunbeams come.—URNER.

Wherefore do I take my flesh in my teeth, and put my life in mine hand? Though he slay me, yet will I trust in him.

That virtue which knows not the utmost that Vice promises to her followers, and rejects it, is but a blank virtue. He that can apprehend and consider Vice, with all her baits and seeming pleasures, and yet abstain and yet prefer that which is truly better, he is the true wayfaring Christian.—MILTON.

The combat.—Jesus, when like ocean billows,
    Fierce temptations on me roll;
  When they sweep me to the breakers,
    Be the anchor of my soul.—KENNEDY.

Whoso looks well upon Great Grace's face, shall see those scars and cuts that shall easily give demonstration of what I say. Yea, once I heard that he should say, and that when he was in the combat: ' We despaired even of life.' How did these sturdy rogues and their fellows make David groan, mourn, and roar! Yea, Heman and Hezekiah too, though champions in their day, were forced to bestir them when by these assaulted, and yet, notwithstanding, they had their coats soundly brushed by them. Peter upon a time would go try what he could do; but though some do say of him that he is the Prince of the Apostles, they handled him so, that they made him at last afraid of a sorry girl. Besides, their king is at their whistle, he is never out of hearing, and if at any time they be put to the worst, he if possible comes in to help them, and of him it is said Job 41. —The sword of him that layeth at him cannot hold, spear, dart, nor harbegeon—esteemeth iron as straw, brass as rotten wood. The arrow cannot make him flee. Sling stones are turned with him into stubble; he laugheth at the shaking of a spear.—BUNYAN.

> Sorrow is knowledge; they, who know the most,
> Must mourn the deepest o'er the fatal truth,
> The tree of knowledge is not that of life.
> *   *   *   *   *   *
> Wait, till like me, your hopes are blighted—till
> Sorrow and shame are handmaids of your cabin;
> Famine and poverty, your guests at table;
> Despair, your bed-fellow—then rise, but not
> From sleep, and judge.—BYRON.

17. Patient and collected souls come out of great trials girt with immortal strength. Such are able to wrestle, not simply against flesh and blood, but against principalities, against powers, against the

rulers of the darkness of this world, and against spiritual wickedness in the aerial regions.

There is an inner circle of faith and brotherhood, occupied by those only who have been tried by fire.— JENKINS.

Not only knowledge, but also every other gift, which we call the gifts of fortune, have power to puff up earth: afflictions only level those mole-hills of pride, plough the heart, and make it fit for wisdom to sow her seed, and for grace to bring forth her increase.—BACON.

Then the blows of time and fate will leave on our souls not disfiguring scars, but inserted buds, innoculating us to bear diviner fruit.—ALGER.

While he thus indulged his grief, a clear and solemn voice, close beside him pronounced these words in the sonorous tone of the readers of the mosque:— Adversity is like the period of the former and of the latter rains,—cold, comfortless, unfriendly to man and to animal ; yet from thence come the flower and the fruit, the date, the rose, and the pomegranate.— W. SCOTT.

For by the sadness of the countenance the heart is made better.

18. Nothing better holds up the mirror to nature, than a letter from a competent pen, written in the fullest freedom of familiarity and the fervor of friendship. He puts on no airs, while he spontaneously does his best. Letters, therefore, by men of parts to

men whom they love and honor, are apt to reveal the
highest reach of their genius.'

Ike Marvel says, Blessed be letters: they are the
monitors, they are also the comforters and they are
the only true heart-talkers.   Of conversation, he says,
the truest thought is modified by a look, a sign, a
sneer, a gesture.   It is not individual, it is not inte-
gral: it is social and mixed.   It is not so with letters.
In them your soul is measuring itself by itself; and
saying its own sayings; there are no sneers to modify
its utterance, no scowl to scare : nothing is present
but you and your thoughts.'

19. What then is the charm, the irresistible charm
of Walpole's writings ?   It consists, we think, in the
art of amusing without exciting.   He never con-
vinces the reason ; nor fills the imagination, nor
touches the heart, but he keeps the mind of the
reader constantly attentive and constantly entertained.   His style is one of those peculiar styles by
which everybody is attracted, and which nobody can
safely venture to imitate.   No man who has written
so much is so seldom tiresome.   He rejects all but
the attractive parts of his subject—no digressions,
unreasonable descriptions, or long speeches.—MA-
CAULAY.

Very few writers make an extraordinary figure in
the world who have not something in their way of
thinking or expressing themselves, that is peculiar to
them, and entirely their own.—SPECTATOR.

Insist on yourself: never imitate. Your own gift you can present every moment with the cumulative force of a whole life's cultivation; but of the adopted talent of another you have only an extemporaneous half-possession. That which each can do best, none but his Maker can teach him. No man yet knows what it is, nor can, till that person has exhibited it. Where is the master who could have taught Shakespeare? Where is the master who could have instructed Franklin, or Washington, or Bacon, or Newton? Every great man is a unique.—EMERSON.

Thomson.—As a writer, he is entitled to one praise of the highest kind: his mode of thinking and expressing his thoughts is original. His blank verse is no more the blank verse of Milton, or of any other poet, than the rhymes of Prior are the rhymes of Cowley. His numbers, his pauses, his diction are of his own growth, without transcription, without imitation. He thinks in a peculiar train, and he thinks always as a man of genius: he looks round on Nature and on Life, with an eye which Nature bestowed only on a poet, the eye which distinguishes in everything presented to its view, whatever there is on which imagination can delight to be detained, and with a mind that at once comprehends the vast, and attends to the minute. The reader of the Seasons wonders that he never saw before what Thomson shows him, and that he never yet has felt what Thomson impresses.—JOHNSON.

Robertson preserved his independence of thought. He had a strong idiosyncrasy, and he let it loose within the bounds of law,—a law not imposed upon him from without by another, but freely chosen by himself as the best. He developed, without rejecting the help of others, his own character after his own fashion. He respected his own conscience, believed in his own native force, and in the divine fire within him. He endeavored to receive, without the intervention of commentators, immediate impressions from the Bible. To these impressions he added the individual life of his own heart, and his knowledge of the life of the great world. He preached these impressions, and with a freedom, independence, variety, and influence which were the legitimate children of his individuality. That men should, within the necessary limits, follow out their own character, and refuse to submit themselves to the common mould, is the foremost need of the age in which we live.—BROOKE.

For we cannot but speak the things which we have seen and heard.

20. The one serious and formidable thing in nature is a will. Society is servile from want of will. —EMERSON.

The majority of men in every age are superficial in character, and brittle in purpose: swarming together in buzzing crowds, in all haunts of amusement, or places of low competition, caring little for anything but low gossip of pastime, the titillation of the senses, and the gratification of conceit. To state the conditions and illustrate the attractions of a holier and grander happiness,—to hold up the examples of nobler characters and lives, lifted into something of loneliness by their gifts and achievements—is accordingly always a timely service. All better lives are so much redeeming leaven kneaded into the lump of humanity.—ALGER.

When the Romans erected a statue to Cato in the Temple of Health, they made upon it no allusion to his victories, but this was the inscription : ' In honor of Cato, the Censor, who, when the Commonwealth was degenerating into licentiousness, by good discipline and wise institutions restored it.' Mr. Stanton, having taught a great lesson in his life, has taught another in his death. He took upon himself, it seems, long since, not only the knightly vow of courage, but the other knightly vow of poverty. Having controlled a national expenditure of two millions a day, he died at last and left his children poor. In those countries where statesmanship means selfishness, this fact alone would prove him no statesman. He would seem to deserve the reproach inflicted by the European statesman on his subordinate—' You are unskilled in the art of fishing in so vast an ocean as the pockets of a hundred million people.'—TRIBUNE.

At the time when Mr. Stanton took the War Office

the country lay in the gentle and complying temper of great officials; the corrupting influences brought to bear upon their personal sensibilities; the concessions made to private claims and impulses at a moment when the opportunities to office and the optional reading of its rules by officials involved the making and losing of vast fortunes for others; when banks, railroad companies, corporations of all kinds, and factories and industrial interests of all sorts, were by those agents, besieging every department of the Government, and using every kind of personal wheedling, and straining every partisan and political nerve to save themselves from ruin, or to avail themselves of some connection with the vast expenditures of the Government to make their fortunes. He was beset alike by the smothering assiduities of the phil anthropic, the unnerving counsels of the timid, the hypocritical proffers of the greedy and the selfish, the insidious claims of personal partiality, the banded conspiracies of industrial corporations or class-interests, the pushing of practiced partisan cliques, the overriding of Congressional committees, the abuse of portions of the public press, the imperfect sympathy of colleagues, the antecedents of the War Office, with the bureaus headed by veteran red tapists; tottering with decorous formality through duties which required the expansive enthusiasm of hopeful youth and teachable manhood—the wide-eyed vision of men born of the great hour.

Were we to anticipate the manners of Sir Charles Grandison, in the man who was to fill a station like this at an hour like that? Not Cerberus himself at the gate of Hades or the mouth of Acheron needed the deep growl, the snarling teeth or the many heads that kept the imprisoned shades in hell, more than the Secretary needed them all to keep imposters, thieves, cowards, and bad advisers out of the War Department, which lead by a short avenue to the Treasury, and by both paths to the breaking heart of the nation.

Beneath Mr. Stanton's robust and stern bosom dwelt a softness and gentleness of heart which made him the idol of his home and the object of a passionate devotion from his personal friends. His external manners were but the rough rind of his tender heart. Rather than against others, he protected himself against himself, the relentings of his gentle spirit, the perilous softenings of his soul by the iron mail of a brusque and cold carriage. Mr. Lincoln! Let his name never be publicly named without honor and reverence, had not a gentler heart, and it was their common tenderness that melted them together and made them one through the war. But Mr. Stanton had a higher mark of greatness because of a diviner type—sadness—the sadness of souls that feel all the loneliness of their unshared responsibility ; the greatness of their ideal shaming their best accomplishments ; their yearning for sympathy back-ed by the necessary, unconquerable superiority and elevation of their views, so that they are dwarfed by the distance they leave others behind them, and made solitary and lonely by the height they attain.

The President was plowed and furrowed with sorrow till his face looked like a sea after a storm when the winds are hushed, but the waves still roll, and the gray clouds make them leaden and sad. But Mr. Stanton's sadness was that of the midnight embers, which shows fire slumbering beneath the ashes—ashes which disappointment, griefs, misunderstandings, abuse, delays, have heaped up, but which, gray and silent, hide unconquerable flames in their bosom.

He was as clear and prompt and all-knowing and omnipotent as Mr. Stewart is in his mercantile establishment. But all his patience of details, his untiring energy and ceaseless labors would have been of little avail without the personal character he brought to the work. Temperate in the extreme he seemed to live from meat and drink unlike that of other men and to keep his body under with almost saintly rigor. He worked when he could not eat, and his invalid hours seemed equal to other men's best. Just so long as the country and the cause required him, he was equal to anything and everything, and postponed sickness, weariness, and almost self-consideration of any kind to the hour when he would not be missed. To his pure hands, up to the arm-pits in the national wealth, there did not stick traitorous one piece of silver.—Bellows.

We have just been reading that simple but wonderful piece ot autobiography entitled : 'Grace abounding to the chief of sinners.' More earnest words were never written. It is the entire unveiling of a human heart, the tearing off of the fig-leaf covering of its sin. The voice which speaks to us from these old pages seems not so much that of a denizen of the world in which we live, as that of a soul at the last solemn confessional. Shorn of all ornament, simple and direct as the contrition and prayer of childhood, when for the first time the Spectre of Sin stands by its bedside; the style is that of a man dead to self-gratification, careless of the world's opinion, and only desirous to convey to others, in all truthfulness and sincerity, the lesson of his inward trials, temptations, sins, weaknesses, and dangers; and to give glory to Him who had mercifully led him through all, and enabled him like his own Pilgrim to leave behind the valley of the Shadow of Death, the Snares of the Enchanted Ground, and the terrors of Doubting Castle, and to reach the Land of Beulah, where the air was sweet and pleasant, and the birds sang, and the flowers sprang up around him, and the Shining Ones walked in the brightness of the not distant Heaven.

He gives no dates; he affords scarcely a clew to his localities; of the man, as he worked, and ate, and drank, and lodged; of his neighbors and contemporaries, of all he saw and heard, of the world about him, we have only an occasional glimpse here and there, in his narrative. It is the story of his inward life only that he relates. What had time and place to do with one who trembled always with the awful consciousness of an immortal nature, and about whom fell alternately the shadows of hell, and the splendors of heaven? We gather indeed from his record, that he was not an idle on-looker in the time of England's great struggle for freedom, but a soldier of the Parliament, in his younger years among the praying sworders and psalm-singing pikemen, the Great-Hearts and Hold-fasts, whom he has immortalized in his allegory; but the only allusion he makes in this portion of experience, is by way of illustration of the goodness of God in preserving him on occasions of peril.—WHITTIER.

22. 'The soul does not get its royal affections, its blessed insights, its sweetness of sensibility and sympathy, its heroic enthusiasm, its great joy in purity and truth, from any mere acquaintance with counsels and commentaries. There are depths which a man must fathom, heights which he must ascend, battles which he must fight, realities of the invisible world which he must experience before he can largely and truly interpret the lovely and awful beauty, and rich and majestic fullness of Christ. He can come into sacred intimacy of souls only through the door of Christ's inspiring brotherhood. To command their confidence he must have wrestled with their temptations, quivered with their sufferings.'

I appeal to the recollection of any man who has passed through that hour of agony, and stood upon the rock at last, the surges stilled below him, and the last cloud lifted from the sky above, with a faith, hope, and trust, no longer traditional but of his own—a trust which neither earth nor hell shall shake thenceforth forever.—ROBERTSON.

'Invisible truth is stronger than indisputable appearances.'

Proof. That which is born of the flesh, is flesh; and that which is born of the Spirit, is Spirit.

Nicodemus answered and said unto him, How can these things be?

Put yourself in communication with the truth, all non-conductors removed, and you will find the action of the Spirit. Apply the philosophy of our great American teacher. When Dr. Franklin would prove the reality of his supposition that electricity was the same as lightning. 'If I can put myself in communication with the charged cloud, the next thunder storm I shall know it.' Accordingly he made his preparations; he prepared his kite, and set the connections as far as in him lay, and with the key at his knuckles waited for the lightning. And the whole world knows the result—how the flash came into his own frame, thrilling his soul with one of the grandest discoveries in science. Just suppose that this had been a spiritual experiment, and Franklin deliberately trying it in prayer, and putting his own soul in communication with God by the Divine Spirit, and had thus become instructed and empowered with an experimental knowledge of spiritual things. But if he had made a Poor Richard's Almanac on those same principles taught him by the Spirit, and had gone forth to proclaim them to the multitude, it would have been to them as another ' morn risen on midnoon.' Set yourself in connection with Divine Truth, removing every disconnecting object and influence as far as in you lies, and lift up your heart to heaven waiting for the Spirit, and you will feel this lightning within you. Put yourself believingly in connection with God, and God will speak to you. Make the experiment your own to see if God's word is true, and God will show it to you. He gave you his truth to be thus experimented upon. Prove me in it, he says, and see if I be not faithful. ' Ye have departed from me and not I from you.'—CHEEVER.

' The early Church were men of like passions with ourselves : they doubted not that prayer had opened and shut the heavens above Ahab's thirsty fields when Elijah had knelt before God: but praying in concert for Peter's deliverance from prison, no apparition could have startled these good Christians more than Peter at their gate: rather than admit their petition granted, they were ready to pronounce the portress mad, or the person knocking ' a spirit.' '

A solitary pilgrim was traversing the desert, retracing the route of his grandfather, a century and a half before. He was on the common highway of travel, which followed for the most part the high stony lands constituting the ' backbone of Palestine.' ' The sun went down; the night gathered; the hard ground was strewn with wide sheets of bare rock; here and there stood up isolated fragments, like ancient Druidical monuments. Here he lay down to rest; and in the visions of the night the rough stones formed themselves into a vast staircase, reaching unto the depth of the starry sky, which, in that wide and open space, without interruption of tent or tree, stretched over the sleeper's head. On that staircase were seen ascending and descending the messengers of God, and from above there came the Divine voice.' —STANLEY.

We can readily understand Jacob's emotion at awaking, when with the evidence that God had, unknown to him, been near, he was afraid and said, How dreadful is this place! Though he had seen nobody but friends, had heard nothing but comforts, he was thrilled with awe. So when Peter saw the great draught of fishes, there was no occasion for terror:—but the presence of the Divine Power made his weak flesh and blood shudder and cry: ' Depart from me, for I am a sinful man, O Lord.' Though this supernatural favor was not in the least deserved, it was beyond question needed. Jacob, troubled with his sins, as he dropped into a tired slumber, feared God had revoked the word spoken to his fathers, and no sound could have been so grateful as the confirmation he heard from above, that he should inherit the land, that his descendants should be immensely numerous, and, that among them one should be a blessing to ' all the families of the earth.'

When believers are in emergencies, the sky opens and down drop promises and celestial friends sent forth to minister for them who shall be heirs of salvation. Little of the powers of the world to come we feel, content and interested among our associates; but in a lull like that of Jacob's bivouac, we see and hear more than we ever dreamed of. Preternatural experiences come when they are needed and can be appreciated. . . To make our pilgrimage joyous, our upward journey easy, and our hearts light, we should obtain interviews with God.—PARK.

26. ' We as yet know but little of the constitution of our own nature. Our consciousness has hardly penetrated beneath the surface of our being. Our deepest and most instructive experiences are only so many explorations of the unknown heritage of mind and soul with which we are endowed. What we have already learned gives us suggestive intimations concerning the unexplained remainder. We must conclude that our minds are not limited by our present and partially developed consciousness, that we have outlying provinces of activity and capacity bordering everywhere upon the unknown infinite. We know that our immaterial nature is open to the beneficent

approach of ministering spirits : we. are even obliged to wrestle against princedoms and powers : and certainly the Almighty Father has not hedged in our spiritual nature by barriers unsurmountable even by Himself.'

So too, God becomes increasingly our God as he is omnipotent, as close to the soul in his habitual action as in his less usual gift.

We believe that a deeper sense of the natural would be much truer to the facts that the time draws near when God shall discover himself much more intimately and tenderly to us than he now does in the hourly shaping and ongoing of what we term Nature, of the universe, which gives the conditions of our being, and brings close home to us the thoughts, the love, the ways of God.

The open eye. has no occasion to search for God, the facts of His being so pour in upon it. Our nature, such as it is, is the abiding fact of this life ; and God's grace works on it as the material which is not to be shifted or escaped, or even complemented by a new loan from Heaven, but which is to be wrought up into Christian character. Many seem to think that all· this is to be changed by death ; that the knot which could not in life be untied is then to be cut ; that the solution of the problem is to· be shirked, and that what Nature, aided by grace, has not done, the supernatural will abundantly do : that the Kingdom of Heaven is, at last, to be vaulted into with· a sudden leap. We are afraid of a supernaturalism so handled, so trusted in, made in this fashion the scapegoat of our indolence and sin. We believe in an omnipotent supernaturalism, but one that is breathed, as the breath of life into Nature, like that breath that made of Adam a living soul.—BASCOM.

'The only greatness worth the name, is the greatness of achievement. With this grandest lesson of history before their eyes, and with the open Bible in their hands, it is passing strange how little conception many Christians have of the achievements possible in the matter of personal religious culture. They are like blind travelers walking through a gold mine, with scanty food for to-day in their knapsacks, but with no idea of the untold opulence lying all around them.'

Take away all the detestable things and I will put a new spirit within you—an heart of flesh—and they shall be my people and I will be their God.

All this is to be learned, experienced, and practised within, by careful and constant attention to our individual consciousness ; which has its laws of disturbances and influences, and its capacities for discipline, regulation, advancement, and purification. And it is to the great field of human labor we must look for religious advancement of the human family.—HALLOWELL.

28. *Old Age.*—*Even to hoar hairs will I carry you.*

An old, old man, with beard as white as snow.—SPENSER.

What is the worst of woes that wait on age?
What stamps the wrinkle deepest on the brow?
To view each loved one blighted from life's page,
    And be alone on earth—as I am now.—BYRON.

. . . . Those tones of dear delight,
The morning welcome, and the sweet good-night.
                —SPRAGUE.

Can gold remove the mortal hour?
In life, can love be bought with gold?
Are friendship's pleasures to be sold?—JOHNSON.

As a man advances in life, he gets what is better than admiration,—judgment to estimate things at their true value.—JOHNSON.

Johnson, now in his seventieth year said, ' it is a man's own fault, it is from want of use, if his mind grows torpid in old age. An old man does not lose faster than he gains, if he exerts himself.'

If the soul aspires for pure and perfect liberty, it also aspires for everything that is noble in Truth, holy in Virtue. The soul never grows old: the eye of age can take in the impression of Beauty with the same enthusiastic joy which leaped through the heart of childhood.—BAYARD TAYLOR.

1. *October.*—' And all the air a solemn stillness holds.'

I stand alone upon the peaceful summit of this hill, and turn in every direction. The east is all aglow; the blue north flushes all her hills with radiance; the west stands in burnished armor; the southern hills buckle the zone of the horizon together with emeralds and rubies, such as were never set in

the fabled girdle of the gods! Of gazing there can
not be enough. The hunger of the eye grows by
feeding.—BEECHER.

> Spendthrift October, art thou wise,
>   Who wastest in thy plenteous prime,
> More beauty on the earth and skies,
> More hue and glow than would suffice
>   To brighten all the winter time?
>
> Yes—better autumn all delight,
>   And then a winter all unblest,
> Than months of mingled dark and light,
> Of faded tints and pallid light,
>   Imperfect dreams and broken rest.
>
> This doubt and dread which naught consoles,
>   Which marks our brows ere manhood's prime:
> This dark uncertainty which rolls
> Like chariot wheels across our souls
>   And makes us old before our time.
>
> So pour your light, October skies,
>   Oh fairest skies which ever are!
> Put on, O Earth, your bravest dyes,
>   And smile although the cricket cries
> And winter threatens from afar.

2. From Salt Lake City to Washoe and the Sierra
Nevada Mountains, the road lies through the most
horrible desert conceivable by the mind of man.
For the sand of the Sahara, we find substituted an
impalpable powder of alkali—white as the driven
snow, stretching for miles at a time one uninterrupted
dazzling sheet which supports not even that last ob-
stinate vidette of civilization—the wild sage bush.

Its springs are far between and without a single ex-
ception mere receptacles of a salt potash and sulphur
hell-broth, which no man would drink save *in extre-
mis*. A few days of this beverage within, and of
wind-drifted alkali invading every pore of the body
without. . . I look back on that desert as the
most frightful night-mare of my existence.

We came into glorious forests of ever-living green;
a rainbow affluence of flowers, an air like a draught
from windows left open in heaven, a crystal sheet of
water fresh-distilled from the snow-peaks, its granite
bottom visible from the depth of a hundred feet, its
banks, a celestial garden lying in a basin thirty-five
miles long, by ten wide, nearly seven thousand feet
above the Pacific lave. Here we sat down to rest,
feeling that one short hour, one little league had
translated us out of the infernal world into heaven.
—BOWLES.

Yosemite.—This vast, open cathedral, which would
hold fifty millions of worshipers is true to the ancient,
imperious maxim of architecture: its mean width
about equals the average height of its walls. Our
eyes now adjusted to its distances were no longer
pained by the amazing spectacle. At last we turned
away from this sublimest page of all the book of nature. I think few can come from its study without
hearts more humble and reverent, lives more worthy
and loyal. The rock mountains are the great feature; indeed, they are Yosemite. The nine granite

walls which range in altitudes from three to six thousand feet are the most striking examples on the globe of the masonry of Nature. Their dimensions are so vast that they utterly outrun our ordinary standards of comparison. One might as well be told of a wall upright like the side of a house for ten thousand miles as for two-thirds of one mile. When we speak of a giant twenty-five feet high, it conveys some definite impression: but to tell of one three thousand feet high, would only bewilder and convey no meaning whatever. So, at first, these stupendous walls painfully confuse the mind. By degrees, day after day, the sight of them clears it, until at last, one receives a just impression of their solemn immensity.—RICHARDSON.

It was in Switzerland that I first felt how constantly to contemplate sublime creation develops the poetic power. It was here that I first began to study nature. Those forests of black, gigantic pines, rising out of the deep snows; those tall, white cataracts, leaping like headstrong youth into the world, and dashing from their precipices, as if allured by the beautiful delusion of their own rainbow mist; those mighty clouds sailing beneath my feet, or clinging to the bosoms of the dark-green mountains, or boiling up like a spell from the invisible and unfathomable depths; the fell avalanche, fleet as a spirit of evil, terrific when its sound suddenly breaks upon the almighty silence, scarcely less terrible when we gaze upon its crumbling and pallid frame varied only by the presence of one or two blasted firs : the head of a mountain loosening from its brother peaks, rooting up in the roar of its rapid rush, a whole forest of pines, and covering the earth for miles with ele-phantine masses ; the supernatural extent of land-scape that opens to us new worlds ; the strong eagles, and the strange wild birds that suddenly cross you in your path, and stare, and shrieking fly—and all the soft sights of joy and loveliness that mingle with these sublime and savage spectacles, the rich pastures, and the numerous flocks, and the golden bees, and the wild flowers, and the carved and painted cottages, and the simple manners and the primæval grace—wherever I moved, I was in turn appalled or enchant-cd ; but whatever I beheld, new images ever sprang up in my mind, and new feelings ever crowded on my fancy.—DISRAELI.

4. *The imagination.*—Its second and ordinary use is to empower us to traverse the scenes of all other history, and force the facts to become again visible, so as to make upon us the same impression which they would have made if we had witnessed them ; and in the minor necessities of life, to enable us out of any present good, to gather the utmost measure of en-joyment by investing it with happy associations, and, also, to give to all mental truths some visible type in allegory, simile, or personification, which shall more deeply enforce them ; and finally, when the

mind is utterly outwearied, to refresh it with such innocent play as shall be most in harmony with the
suggestive voices of natural things, permitting it to
possess living companionship instead of silent beauty.
These being the uses of imagination, its abuses are
either in creating for mere pleasure, false images,
where it is its. *duty* to create true ones, or in turning
what was intended for the mere refreshment of the
heart into its daily food, and changing the innocent
pastimes of an hour into the guilty occupation of a
life.

It is said that modern science is averse to the
exercise and development of the imaginative faculty.
But is it really so ?   Are visions such as those in
which we have been indulging less richly charged
with that poetic pabulum on which fancy feeds and
grows strong, than those ancient tales of enchant-
ment and *faery* which beguiled of old in solitary
homesteads, the long winter nights ? Because science
flourishes must poesy decline ? The complaint seems
but to betray the weakness of the class who urge it.
True, in an age like the present,—considerably more
scientific than poetical,—science substitutes for the
smaller poetry of fiction, the great poetry of truth :
and as there is a more general interest felt in new
revelations of what God has wrought, than in exhibitions of what the humbler order of poets have half-
borrowed, half-invented, the disappointed dreamers
complain that the 'material laws' of science have

pushed them from their place. As well might the Arab who prided himself upon the beauty of some white tent which he had reared in some green oasis of the desert, complain of the dull tools of Belzoni's laborers, when engaged in clearing from the sands, the front of some august temple of the ancient time. It is not the tools, it might well be said to the complainer, that are competing with your neat little tent: it is the sublime edifice hitherto covered up, which the tools are laying bare. Nor is it the material laws, we may on the same principle say to the poets of the querulous cast, that are overbearing your little inventions; but those sublime works and wonderful actings of the Creator which they unveil and bring into comparison with yours. But from His works and His actings have the masters of the lyre ever derived their choicest materials; and whenever a truly great poet arises—one that will add a profound intellect to a powerful imagination,—he will find science not his enemy, but an obsequious caterer and a devoted friend. What is it, let me ask, that imparts · to Nature its poetry? It is not in Nature itself: it resides not either in dead or organized matter,—in rock, or bird, or flower: 'the deep saith it is not in me, and the sea saith it is not in me.' It is in mind that it lives and breathes: external nature is but its storehouse of subjects and models, and it is not till these are called in as images, and invested with 'the light that never was on land or sea,' that they cease to be of the earth, earthy, and form the etherial stuff of which the visions of poets are made. Nay, is it not mainly through that associative faculty to which the sights and sounds of present nature become suggestive of the images of a nature not present, but seen within the mind that the landscape pleases, or that we find beauty in its woods or beside its streams, or the impressive and sublime among its mountains and its rocks? Nature is a vast tablet inscribed with signs, each of which has its own significancy, and becomes poetry in the mind when read; and geology is simply the key by which myriads of these signs, hitherto undecipherable, can be unlocked and perused, and thus a new province added to the poetical domain.—HUGH MILLER.

Scottish poetry is the poetry of Home, of Nature, and the Affections. All this is sadly wanting in our young literature. We have no songs. American domestic life has never been hallowed and beautified by the sweet, and graceful, and tender associations of poetry. We have no Yankee pastorals. Our rivers and streams turn mills and float rafts, and are otherwise as commendably useful as those of Scotland: but no quaint ballad or simple song reminds us that men and women have loved, met and parted on their banks, or that beneath each roof within those valleys, the tragedy and comedy of life has been enacted. Our poetry is cold and imitative: it seems more the product of overstrained intellects, than the spontaneous, outgushing of hearts warm with love, and strongly sympathizing with human nature as it actually exists about us, with the joys and griefs of the men and women we meet daily. Who shall say that we have not the essential of the poetry of human life and simple nature, of the hearth, and the farm-field? Here then is a mine unworked, a harvest ungathered. Who shall sink the shaft, and thrust in the sickle? And here let us say that the mere dilletante and the amateur ruralist may as well keep their hands off. The prize is not for them. He who would successfully strive must be himself what he sings,—part and parcel of the rural life of New England; one who has grown strong amidst its healthful influences, familiar with all its details, and capable of detecting whatever of beauty, humor, or pathos pertain to it.—WHITTIER.

The grand difference between a Dryasdust and a sacred poet is very much even this: To distinguish well what does still reach to the surface, and is alive and frondent for us : and what reaches no longer to the surface, but moulders safe under ground, never to send forth leaves and fruit for mankind any more. When both oblivion and memory are wise, when the general soul of man is clear, melodious, true, there may come a modern Iliad as memorial of the Past.—CARLYLE.

We have been eighty years an organized nation, ninety-three years an independent people, more than two hundred years an American race, and to-day, for the first time in our history, we met to dedicate publicly a monument to an American Poet.

The rhythmical expression of emotion, or passion, or thought, is a need of the human race—coëval with speech, universal as religion, the prophetic forerunner as well as the last begotten offspring of civilization. Poetry belongs equally to the impressible childhood of a people, and to the refined ease of their maturity. It is both, the instructive effort of Nature, and the loftiest ideal of Art, receding to farther and farther spheres of spiritual Beauty, as men rise to the capacity of its enjoyment. But our race was transferred half-grown, from the songs of its early ages and the inspiring associations of its Past, and set here, face to face with stern tasks, which left no space for the lighter play of the mind. The early generations of English bards gradually became foreign to us, for their songs, however sweet, were not those of our own home. We profess to claim an equal share in Chaucer, and Spenser, and Shakespeare; but it is a hollow pretence. They belong to our language, but we cannot truly feel that they belong to us as a people. The destiny that placed us on this soil robbed us of the magic of tradition, the wealth of romance, the suggestions of history, the sentiment of inherited homes and customs, and left us shorn of our lisping childhood, to create a poetic literature for ourselves. It is not singular, therefore,

that this Continent should have waited long for its
first-born poet. The intellect, the energy of character, the moral force—even the occasional taste and
refinement,—which were shipped hither from the
older shores, found the hard work of history already
portioned out for them, and the muses discovered no
nook of guarded leisure, no haunt of sweet contemplation, which might tempt them to settle among us.
Labor may be Prayer, but it is not Poetry. Liberty
of Conscience and Worship, practical Democracy,
the union of Civil Order and personal Independence,
are ideas which may warm the hearts and brains of
men, but the soil in which they strike root is too
full of fresh, unsoftened forces to produce the delicate wine of song. The highest product of ripened
intellect cannot be expected in the nonage of a nation.

In the same year in which the Constitution of the
United States was completed and adopted, the first
poet was born—Richard Henry Dana, who still lives
and, despite his gray head, still keeps the freshness
and youth of the poetic nature. Less than three years
after him Fitz-Greene Halleck came into the world—
the lyrical genius following the grave and contempla-
tive muse of his elder brother. In Halleck, therefore,
we mourn our first loss out of the first generation of
American bards; and a deeper significance is thus
given to the personal honors which we lovingly pay
to his memory. Let us be glad, not only that these
honors have been so nobly deserved, but also that we
find in him a fitting representative of his age!

Let us forget our sorrow for the true man, the steadfast friend, and rejoice that the earliest child of song whom we return to the soil that bore him for us, was the brave, bright, and beautiful growth of a healthy, masculine race. No morbid impatience with the restrictions of life, no fruitless lament over an unattainable ideal, no inherited gloom of temperament, such as finds delight in what it chooses to call despair, ever muffled the clear notes of his verse, or touched the sunny cheerfulness of his history. His life offers no enigmas for our solution. Clear, frank, simple, and consistent, his song and his life were woven into one smooth and even thread. We would willingly pardon in him some expression of dissatisfaction with a worldly fate, which, in certain respects, seemed inadequate to his genius, but we find that he never uttered it. The basis of his nature was a knightly bravery, of such firm and enduring temper that it kept from him even the ordinary sensitiveness of the poetic character. From the time of his studies as a boy, in the propitious kitchen which heard his first callow numbers, to the last days of a life which had seen no liberal, popular recognition of his deserts, he accepted his fortune with the perfect dignity of a man who cannot stoop to discontent. During his later visits to New York, the simplest, the most unobtrusive, yet the cheerfullest man to be seen among the throngs of Broadway, was Fitz-Greene Halleck. Yet, with all his simplicity, his

bearing was strikingly gallant and fearless : tne carriage of his head suggested the wearing of a helmet,
the genial frankness and grace of his manner, in his
intercourse with men, has suggested to others the
epithet 'courtly,' but I prefer to call it *manly*, as the
expression of a rarer and finer quality than is usually found in the atmosphere of courts. It is not
necessary that we should attempt to determine his
relative place among American poets. It is sufficient
that he deserves every honor that we can render to
his memory, not only as one of the very first representatives of American Song, but from his intrinsic
quality as a poet. Let us rather be thankful for
every star set in our heaven, than seek to ascertain
how they differ from one another in glory. If any
critic would diminish the loving enthusiasm of those
whose lives have been brightened by the poet's personal sunshine, let him remember that the sternest
criticism will set the lyrics of Halleck higher than
their author's unambitious estimate. A poem which
bears within itself its own right to existence will not
die. Its rhythm is freshly fed from the eternal
pulses of Beauty, whence flows the sweetest life of
the human race. The poetic literature of a land is
the finer and purer ether above its material growth
and the vicissitudes of its history.—BAYARD TAYLOR.

11. Coleridge is rich almost beyond comparison in
euphonious and assonant alliteration. Much of the
wild and weird effect of the 'Ancient Mariner' and

of the mastery of its spell is due to the subtle inter-
linking of the sounds of letters. The fascination is
intensified by the congregation and commingling of
similar vocables and the coloring is thereby deepened.

> The breezes blew, the white foam flew,
>   The furrow followed free :
> We were the first that ever burst
>   Into that silent sea.

Once more—

> And the coming wind did roar more loud,
> And the sails did sigh like sedge.—RURAL NEW YORKER.

12. I have somewhere read of an eminent person,
who used in his private offices of devotion to give
thanks to Heaven that he was born a Frenchman :
for my part I look upon it as a peculiar blessing that
I was born an -Englishman. Among many other
reasons I think myself very happy in my country, as
the language of it is wonderfully adapted to a man
who is sparing of his words, and an enemy to loqua-
city. The English delight in silence more than any
other European nation, if the remarks made on us by
foreigners are true.

This humor shows itself, first of all by its abound-
ing in monosyllables, which gives us an opportunity
of delivering our thoughts in few sounds. This indeed takes off from the elegance of our tongue, but
expresses our ideas in the readiest manner, and con-
sequently answers the first design of speech better
than the multitude of syllables, which make the

words of other languages more tunable and sonorous. In the next place we may observe that where the words are not monosyllables, we often make them so, by our rapid pronunciation,—which has turned a tenth part of our smoothest words into so many clusters of consonants. . . There is another particular in our language which is a great instance of our frugality of words, and that is the suppressing of several particles which must be produced in other tongues to make a sentence intelligible; this often perplexes the best writers, when they find the relatives, whom, which, or they, at their mercy, whether they may have admission or not; and will never be decided until we have something like an academy, that by the best authorities and rules drawn from the analogy of languages shall settle all controversies between grammar and idiom.—ADDISON.

There is for every thought a certain nice adaptation of words, which none other could equal, and which when a man has been so fortunate as to hit, he has attained the perfection of language.—BOSWELL.

It is now the accepted doctrine of philologists that thought is impossible, beyond the most rudimentary limits, without signs, through which we not only communicate with our fellows, but slowly climb ourselves, from round to round of conception, till our whole intellectual fabric is built up. The development of intelligence is the development of its symbols; for every emotion, however fugitive and deli-

10

cate, is born in the word which thereaterf becomes its home,—the obedient, docile, ever-ready word,— the sound so flexible that it bends to each whim and caprice of its master's bidding, and yet so firm and infixed in the very soul of things that it outlasts the mountains and the stars.

Art, by the spontaneous play of fantasy, discerns the most subtle, remote, recondite, and unsuspected analogies between things which have nothing in common, not even existence, and out of them evokes a gorgeous corruscation that, like an aurora, fills the whole sky with splendor; but, unlike the aurora, once kindled will never fade.—GODWIN.

Intellect in any science is indicated by classification and arrangement. Accent is the subordination of inferior things to superior—gives predominance to leading thoughts—what mountains are to the globe, and fixed stars to the planets. The more refined the accent, the more cultured the intellect. An idiot jumbles. A person in low spirits, or in a loose and unhinged state of mind, moans and monotones : keyed up and excited, he defines and analyzes by accent. The higher the intellectual refinement, the keener the appreciation of words, the broader and minuter is the poet's domain in all the fine shades of thought —BARTLETT.

14. *Genius.*—An organization so sensitive that it easily goes into a state of exaltation and produces results more fruitful than can be produced by ordinary means.—BEECHER.

Genius pertains always and exclusively to the moral nature. Spiritual *sympathy* is its very atmosphere. But this sympathy in some men is so entirely occupied and absorbed in an ideal world, and is so exclusively directed toward goals that are only discerned by the highest order of prophetic instinct, that it scarcely touches the individual heart: its appeal is to the race. Our Platos operate by cycles—through the attraction of gravitation, rather than through the molecular affinities. This perhaps is the highest order of human power; it is certainly the grandest. But there is another kind of genius that does not elevate itself above the immediate circle of its movement, but which most strongly allies itself with the moral forces with which it comes in contact.— CURTIS.

Mr. Raymond's official career, though evincing ability, did less than justice to his comprehensive knowledge and rare intellectual powers. Never so positive and downright in his convictions as his countrymen are apt to be, he was often misjudged as a trimmer and time-server, when, in fact, he spoke and wrote exactly as he felt and thought. If what he uttered to-day was not in full accordance with what he said yesterday, the difference evinced in his essay was a true reflection of one which had preceded it in his mind.—GREELEY.

The secret of genius is to suffer no fiction to exist for us; to realize all that we know, in the high re-

finement of modern life, in arts, in sciences, in books,
in men; to exact good faith, reality, and a purpose;
and first, last, midst, and without end, to honor every
truth by use.—EMERSON.

> ' A life impetuous with desire
>   To battle on the plains of Right :
> A quick brain kindling tongues of fire
>   To light the torch on Freedom's height.'

Ode to Genius.—All things tremble, all things bow
   Before thy awfully majestic brow
   Save Goodness; Cowardice and gloomy Fear
   Shrink backward, cowering from thy look severe,
        One burning glance,
        One leveled lance
        From that sunbeamy eye,
        And Bribery and Avarice,
        Grim Tyranny and Prejudice,
        And Wrong and Folly fly ;
   And Pride and dull Pretension melt away,
   Like night before the golden wheels of day.

Like Israel's glorious leader thou dost stretch
   Thy wand across the rushing tide of years
And roll it back, and from its chambers fetch
   To life its lovely wrecks and smiles and tears.

        The fiery secrets of the universe
            Come to thy call—
        The glorious generations
Of former worlds leap from their marble graves
            And unto thee rehearse
        The mighty poem of the lost creations.
                              —HEMPSTEAD.

Out from the heart of nature rolled
The burdens of the Bible old.
The litanies of nations came
Like the volcano's tongue of flame:
Up from the burning core below,
The canticles of love and woe.
The hand that rounded Peter's dome,
And groined the aisles of Christian Rome,
Wrought in sad sincerity,
Himself from God he could not free.
He builded better than he knew,
The conscious stone to beauty grew.
Know'st thou what wove you wood-bird's nest
Of leaves and feathers from her breast?
Or how the fish outbuilt her shell,
Painting with morn each annual cell?
Or how the sacred pine-tree adds
To his old trees new myriads?
Such and so grew these holy piles,
Whilst love and terror laid the tiles.—EMERSON.

*Or speak to the earth and it shall teach thee, and
the fishes of the sea shall declare it unto thee. Who
knoweth not in all these that the hand of the Lord hath
wrought this?*

16. Wisdom is the gift of God, who told Moses
that he had filled with wisdom and understanding
and knowledge Bezaleel and Aholiah, to invent and
perform several sorts of work for completing the
tabernacle. It was this sort of wisdom that Solomon
entreated of God with so much earnestness, and
which God granted him with great liberality.

As for these four children, God gave them know-

*ledge and skill in all learning and wisdom: and
Daniel had understanding in all visions and dreams.*

Or rapt Isaiah's wild, seraphic fire.—BURNS.

For mine eyes have seen the King, the Lord of hosts.

17. It is not the amount which is poured in, that
gives wisdom, but the amount of creative mind and
heart working on, and stirred by, what is so poured
in.—BEECHER.

To Foster a text of Scripture suggested more sublime thoughts than could ever be suggested from the
prolixity of Gill, or even from the simple piety of
Henry. . . He combined with mechanical labors
the severest application to study, frequently spending
great part of many a night in reading and in those
prolonged meditations which furnished him with a
key to the secret and deep places of mind; providing
that microscopic species of perception which detects
whole realms of life where others see but a tame,
dead level.—SHARPE'S MAGAZINE.

> The lamp of genius tho' by nature lit,
> If not protected, prun'd and fed with care,
> Soon dies, or runs to waste with fitful glare.—WILCOX.

Buckle.—His first real power was shown in the
game of chess, in which he had made an European
name before he was twenty years old. During his
stay on the Continent the idea of his great work first
dawned upon his mind. As the thought expanded
his sense of power increased, and the faculty of ori-

ginal speculation sprang into life. His desultory studies were now co-ordinated to one definite purpose. He conceived the gigantic project of setting forth in one connected view the various paths by which the human intellect has won the fullness and freedom which we call civilization, seeking through the records of history for the same empire of law in the march of human progress which physical science discloses in the material universe. No man was ever so fully prepared for labor on so extensive a field. He ranged over extensive provinces of science in order to master every fruitful principle to trace the influence of philosophical methods on the progress of knowledge, and thus to find the basis of those wide generalizations which underlie his theory. Within those limits there was perhaps no branch of science which he had not studied, of which he had not followed the history and tracked the important threads of discovery. In metaphysical research—his purpose was the same. From the earliest Greek to the latest German, he read with the aim of seizing in each system the master-thought which had shaped the practical philosophy or political life of nations. In literature, he did not seek for mere scholarship, but to trace the development of intellect through the forms of different languages and different social conditions. For this purpose he had made himself acquainted with most of the languages of Europe.— TRIBUNE.

Human wisdom is the fruit of intellectual activity and spontaneity: the heavenly wisdom, on the contrary, is an effect of divine influence on man's receptive faculties, and is the root of the life of faith. But while faith belongs altogether to the heart, wisdom, in its heavenly form, is a blossom of the intellect.—OLSHAUSEN.

' Power dwelt in his broad, unwrinkled forehead and pensive eyes—such subtle, mysterious power, as Nature sometimes endows men with, making them royal in a kingdom where to be supreme is to be immortal.'

. . . he belongs to the band of far-shining men of whom Pericless declares the whole world to be the tomb.—MORLEY.

Courage, poor Grandfather: here is a new second edition of a Friedrich, the first having gone off with so little effect: this one's back is still unbroken, his life's seed-field not yet filled with tares and thorns; who knows but Heaven will be kinder to this one? Heaven was much kinder to this one. Him Heaven had kneaded of more potent stuff: a mighty fellow this one, and a strange—related to the Sphere-harmonies, and the divine and demonic Powers; of a swift, far-darting nature this one, like an Apollo clad in sun-beams and in lightnings (after his sort,) and with a back which all the world could not succeed in breaking. Yes, if, by most rare chance, this was indeed a new man of genius, born into the purblind, rotten century, in the acknowledged rank of a king there—man of genius, that is to say, man of originality and veracity, capable of seeing with his eyes, and incapable of not believing what he sees. Then, truly.—CARLYLE.

21. *Simplicity.*—Chatham had one fault, which of all human faults is most rarely found in company with true greatness. He was extremely affected. He was an almost solitary instance of a man of real genius, and of a brave, lofty, and commanding spirit, without simplicity of character.—MACAULAY.

De Witt.—His simplicity and openness amazed Temple, who had been accustomed to the affected solemnity of his patron, the Secretary, and to the eternal doublings and evasions which passed for great feats of statesmanship among the Spanish politicians at Brussels. ' Whoever,' he wrote to Arlington, 'deals with M. De Witt, must go the same plain way—without refining, or coloring, or offering shadow for substance.' He was scarcely less struck by the modest dwelling and frugal table of the first citizen of the richest state in the world. While Clarendon was amazing London with a dwelling more sumptuous than the palace of his master, while Arlington was lavishing his ill-gotten wealth on the decoys and orange gardens and interminable conservatories of Euston,—the great statesman who had frustrated all their plans of conquest, and the roar of whose guns they had heard with terror even in the

10*

galleries of Whitehall, kept only a single servant, walked about the streets in the plainest garb, and never used a coach, except for visits of ceremony.— MACAULAY.

22. Sorrow.—' Till ₁rom the straw the flail the corn doth beat,
    Until the chaff be purged from the wheat;
    Yea, till the mill the grains in pieces tear,
    The richness of the flour will scarce appear.'

Oh, let us thank God for the love and sorrow of genius! Yet let us thank him reverently, as we thank him for all the blessings which come to us, by the sacrifice and pains of others. We take the flowers that blossom from the thorny stems, but they long for the time when the Master's eye shall see that the fruit is ripe, and his hand shall gather it in. —GARRETT.

Is not this the blood of the men that went in jeopardy of their lives ?—therefore he would not drink it but poured it out unto the Lord.

25. *Though I be rude in speech.*—

The gospel sets no value upon the opulence of talents with which a man may have been endowed, but only upon the disposition of the mind in reference to the will of God. It is the upright only to whom God shows favor. Now this vain ostentation (of Simon's) forms a glaring contrast with the humility of the apostles, who, although really filled with all the powers of the heavenly world, yet most sharply reprehended all undue estimation of their own persons.

They desired to be regarded as nothing but weak instruments, and their illustrious works were designed to glorify not themsclves, but only the eternal God, and his Son.—OLSHAUSEN.

I believe the first test of a truly great man is his humility. I do not mean by humility doubt of his own power, or hesitation in speaking of his opinions : but a right understanding of what he can do and say, and the rest of the world's sayings and dc.ngs. All great men not only know their business, but know that they know it, and are not only right in their main opinions, but they usually know that they are right in them ; only they do not think much cf themselves on that account,—they do not expect their fellow-men therefore to fall down and worship them ; they have a curious under sense of powerlessness, feeling that the greatness is not *in* them, but *through* them.—RUSKIN.

'To be good, to be a genuine philanthropist, a faithful lover of God and man, having virtue grounded upon truth,—this is always better than intellectual splendor. It is folly to sigh for gifts not our own, or envy renown that seeks other names ; yet all may find a place in the temple of virtue, and forever carry the garland of victorious goodness. This really makes the good man—the man whom God honors, and who treads the path of immortal fame.'

'He who trusts in Christ alone,
Not in aught himself hath done
He, great God, shall be thy care,
And thy choicest blessings share.'

12. *Nehemiah's Wall.*—*Now Tobiah said,—Even that which they build, if a fox go up, he shall even break down their stone wall. Hear, our God, for we are despised.*

Help us, our God! while men with keen derision
Mock our slight structure as it riseth up:
Help us our God! despised are we and broken,
By many sorrows that the wicked cause:
Turn thou on them their malice as the token
Of thine unerring, unevaded laws.—DUFFIELD.

For still the world prevailed, and its dread laugh
Which scarce the firm philosopher can scorn.
                                        —THOMSON.

Adroit casuistry in the art of reasoning.

I could not undeceive him on this head; nor what was more, could I satisfy my own conscience that he was altogether in the wrong; for, with a diabolical ingenuity he had contrived to hit on some of the most vexatious doubts which disturbed my mind and instinctively to detect the secret cares and difficulties that beset me. The lesson should never be lost on us that the devil was depicted as a sneerer!—LEVER.

Doth Job fear God for naught?

14. *The Power unseen.*—It is easy to sneer at sentimentalism; it is an old style of sneer. It is easy to represent enthusiasm, idealism, high aims, unselfish purposes, as coming under that name—an old representation. And yet the man who does not know it has been stronger than interest, ideas mightier than armed hosts, belief masterful beyond the power of empires,—the man who does not know and habitually recognize the fact that these things have been the world's destroying and creative forces, is as blind as a mole to human nature and the history of this planet. There have been crises again and again, when wealth, honor, power, all that your Philistine thinks worth striving for—have been flung into the gulf like trash, for the sake of some pure bit of ' sentiment '—aye, even a sentimentalism—an idea preached and propagated by men who do not know where to get their dinners, has the power to sweep the merchant and his warehouses, the banker and his stocks and securities, the alderman and his dinners in a whirlwind away. He knows that these vast unseen powers hold the world at their mercy ; that a word, a name, an idea, the symbol of an idea, a sentiment, a formula embodying it, can crush one social order into chaos, and build another on its ruin : he knows that it has so been a hundred times, and that no man can tell when it may not be again. A word—the symbol of a thought—has consumed strong cities and wasted half a continent. Another such word has built cities in the desert and redeemed half an empty world to human uses. A sentiment, an invisible idea may be gathering force to-day, taught by the tongues and pens of men you may count dreamers, which shall change the earth and sweep all things you think enduring into oblivion five centuries hence. Do not put your trust in your high common-sense, and boasted worldly knowledge ; not in the coat, but in the man, not in the husk, but in the kernel, not in the casket, but in the jewel. It is an old truth, and has a wider sweep than thousands always give it.—' The things which are seen are temporal.'—CHURCHMAN.

For in one hour so great riches is come to naught.

' Truth, loyalty, and self-respect !—you are but thin shades dwelling in the human breast, lightly esteemed, seemingly of little 'power : but when you depart the pillars of the world seem to have fallen in so weak and desolate are our lives without you.'

' A majority in this world are always on the side of that which appeals to the physical senses. But it is in the long reckonings that the spiritual is shown to be in the ascendant.'

Credible to those who reasoned by sentiment, and made syllogisms of their passions, it was incredible then and evermore to the sane and healthy intelligence which in the long run commands the mind or the world. In the long run—yet the force which eventually maintains the ascendency is the slowest in rising to it.—FROUDE.

The race is not to the swift.

The unremitting attention of high sentiments in obscure duties is hardening the character to that temper which will work with honor, if need be, in the tumult or on the scaffold.

There are men who rise refreshed on hearing a threat; men to whom a crisis which intimidates and paralyzes the majority,—demanding not the faculties of prudence and thrift, but comprehension, immovableness, the readiness of sacrifice, comes graceful and beloved as a bride.—EMERSON.

Sir Thomas More.—Seeing that persuasion could not move him, then began they more terribly to threaten him. 'My Lords,' answered he, these tertors be frights for children and not for me.' Thereupon they, with great displeasure dismissed him : and knowing whom (King Henry VIII.) in the defence of his innocence he taunted and defied, he well knew the price he was to pay for his boldness. Nevertheless, he was in high spirits, and taking boat for Chelsea, his son-in-law, Roper, who accompanied him, believed from his merriment by the way, that his name has been struck out from the bill. When they were landed and walking in the garden, Roper said, 'I trust, sir, all is well, you are so merry.' 'It is so, indeed, son, thank God.' 'Are you then, sir, put out of the bill ? ' 'Wouldst thou know, son, why I am so joyful ? In good faith I rejoice that I have given the devil a foul fall; because I have with those lords gone so far, that without great shame I can never go back.' This heartfelt exultation at having, after a struggle to which he felt the weakness of human nature might have been unequal, gained the victory in his own mind, and though with the almost certain sacrifice of life, made it impossible to resile —bestows a greatness on these simple and familiar words which belongs to few uninspired sayings in ancient and modern times.

Whereas he evermore used before at his departure from his wife and children whom he tenderly loved, to have them bring him to his boat, and there to kiss them and bid them farewell—then would he suffer none of them forth at the gate to follow him, and with a heavy heart took boat toward Lambeth. On his way he whispered into the ear of his son-in-law who accompanied him, 'I thank our Lord the field is won,'—indicating an entire confidence in his own constancy. . . His character both in public and private life comes as near to perfection as our nature will permit: and I must think that there has been too much concession on the score that the splendor of his great qualities was obscured by intolerance and superstition: and that he voluntarily sought his death by violating a law which with a safe conscience he might have obeyed. With all my Protestant zeal, I must feel a higher reverence for Sir Thomas More, than for Oliver Cromwell or Cranmer.—CAMPBELL'S CHANCELLORS.

As the noble owner of Warwick's castle enjoyed

his calm retreat surrounded by his family; as he looked from his windows on his broad domain; as he paced the greensward by the gentle Avon and thought of the horrors with which civil conflict might ere long cover that happy scene, it must have been with reluctance though it was with steady heroism that he buckled on the sword.—MACAULAY.

Whatever may be the price you set upon your patrimony, your honor—life: hold yourself in readiness at all times to sacrifice everything to duty, should duty exact such sacrifices from you. Without this abrogation of self, this renunciation of every earthly advantage rather than to retain it by a compact with evil,—a man can show no heroism of character, nay, he may even become a monster! 'For no one,' in the words of Cicero, ' can be just who fears death, sorrow, exile, and poverty, or who prefers those things which are the opposite of these to equity.' To live with feelings alienated from the transitory prosperity by which we are surrounded appears to some persons an impracticable and harsh resolve, almost allied to barbarism. It is nevertheless true that without a timely indifference to these extraneous goods, we neither know how to live or die worthily. In whatever form it may be your destiny to meet death, show a prompt spirit, a dignified courage, and sanctify it with all the sincerity and energy of your faith.—MY SON'S MANUAL.

For more than forty years, I have so ruled my

life that when death came I might face it without fear.—HAVELOCK.

But there is something worse than death. Cowardice is worse. And it is worse than death, aye, worse than a hundred thousand deaths, when a people have gravitated down into a creed that the wealth of a nation consists not in generous hearts, fire in each breast, and freedom on each brow: in national virtues and primitive simplicity and heroic endurance and preference of duty to life.—BEECHER.

'Worldliness,—the most terrific of any vice.'

The mind in which either of those three emotions, viz., the love of liberty, the love of country, and the love of mankind is predominant, will be exalted above the immediate wants of mankind; but if the three noble feelings unite and govern in the same mind, be sure that that individual will be mighty among his race. No matter in what station he is born, to what calling he has been destined—there is that in his own breast which will bear him upward and onward. And the course of conduct which in a man of his character, may at first appear presumptuous or impossible, will in the end be found perfectly consistent with a confidence which a well-balanced and justly discriminating mind should feel in its own strength and resources.'

> 'But he who can back on a true spirit fall,
> No wrong can excite and no danger appal.'

King William III.—One of the most remarkable qualities of this man, ordinarily so saturnine and reserved, was that danger acted on him like wine ; opened his heart, loosened his tongue, and took away all appearance of constraint from his manner. On this memorable day he was seen wherever the peril was the .greatest :—his lieutenants in vain implore him to retire to some station from which he could give his orders, without exposing a life so valuable to Europe.—MACAULAY.

To how many organizations does deadly peril bring the noiseless excitement which chains down every physical disability and injects the ropy veins with unconquerable will, and while wholly detaching the mind from all thought of kindred and care of self, gives it a thousandfold power of observation, of judgment and decision.—TRIBUNE COR.

19. *My heart is toward the governors of Israel, that offered themselves willingly among the people.*

' Without haste, without rest, I forsee a patient dozen or hundred men, lay their plans in this generation and the next—watching undeterred by temporary disaster—it moves in its steady way onward till it reaps the full harvest of a complete success.'

Such souls when they appear are the Imperial Guard of virtue, the perpetual reserve, the dictators of fortune. One needs not praise their courage,— they are the heart and soul of nature. It is in rugged crises, in inweariable endurance, and in aims which put sympathy out of question, that the angel is shown.'—EMERSON.

20. A talent is perfected in solitude: a character in the stream of the world.—GOETHE.

They who will mix with men, and especially they who will govern them must in many things obey them. They who will yield to no such conditions may be hermits, but cannot be generals or statesmen. If a man will walk straightforward without turning to the right or to the left, he must walk in a desert and not in Cheapside. Thus was he enforced to do many things which jumped not with his inclination nor made for his honor.—MACAULAY'S COWLEY AND MILTON.

Friedrich to Voltaire: Would you know my way of life? We march from seven in the morning till four in the afternoon. I dine then: afterward I work. I receive tiresome visits: with these comes a detail of insipid matters of business. 'Tis wrong-headed men punctiliously difficult, who are to be set right; heads too hot which must be restrained; idle fellows that must be urged, impatient men which must be rendered docile, plunderers to be restrained within the boundaries of equity; babblers to hear babbling, dumb people to keep in talk; in fine one has to drink with those that like it, to eat with those that are hungry: One has to become a Jew with Jews and a Pagan with Pagans.—CARLYLE.

22. *And as thy servant was busy here and there he was gone.*

It is the oft-recurring lesson, the forfeiture of solemn trusts through inadvertence ; great neglects, irreparable losses, going on under cover of busy attention to duties here and there.—W. J. B.

Footprints.—In a red sand-stone deposit in the valley of the Connecticut are fossil footprints, made by strange, gigantic birds, living in the time of Lias. These impressions, made before there existed a human mind, even before there lived a single mammalia, exhibit as distinctly every claw and phalange, as when first imprinted on the soft sand, and show a wonderful record to those skilled in reading the petrified hieroglyphics in the diary of the world's creation.

Reader, what footprints are you making? Are you so near a cipher that you may fall out of the ranks unmissed? Unless you are a drone, a nonentity, doing nothing, living for nothing, except to eat, sleep, and die, your footprints will last, keep a record and teach a lesson.—PRESTON.

> Lives of great men all remind us
> We can make our lives sublime,
> And departing leave behind us
> Footprints on the sands of time.
>> —LONGFELLOW.

We can think of no sublimer spectacle within the limits of flesh and blood than that furnished by a great and pure mind, strengthened and adorned by the accumulated knowledge of ages, thrilled with the insperation of its task, eager for its work, exposing error, finding and defending truth, pleading the cause of justice and right, lifting human thought above its usual level; hastening forward the grand march of society, working by night and by day to illumine and bless mankind, and then through the open gates of eternity ascending to the skies.

The bare possibility of achieving such a life ought to stir every mind with the ardors of the most intense enthusiasm. To make a good impression upon the world—an impression that shall not only endure, but descend along the current of ages with expanding and increasing power, by attaching to itself new and auxiliary causes of greatness—is an object which any being may well covet, whether man or angel. A life which attains this object is a grand success. The actor therein has, as he deserves, a place among the Historic Dead.—SPEAR.

> ' I shall be glad that I did work and weep—
> Be glad, O God, my slumbering soul did wake—
> Be glad my stubborn heart did heave and break
> Beneath thy plow—when angels come to·reap.'

Sir Eardly Wilmot.—We must place him far above those who have been tempted by inordinate ambition, to mean or wicked actions; yet we cannot consider his public character as by any means approaching to perfection, for he was much more solicitous for his own ease than for the public good. By becoming a representative of the people, he might have materially assisted the house of Commons in its legislative deliberation. By accepting the great seal he would have rescued the country from the incompetency of Bathurst, who, hardly qualified to be a chairman of Quarter Sessions, presided seven years on the woolsack. Filling the marble chair, what benefits might he not have conferred upon the community by his decisions and by the amendment of our laws! He was deterred not by any misgivings as to his own qualifications, or by any dislike to the political opinions of those with whom he was to be associated in the Cabinet, but by morbid hatred of conspicuous position and by selfish love of tranquillity. He did not shun political strife that he might make discoveries in science, or contribute to the literary fame of his country. The tendency of the tastes by which he was animated is to make life not only inglorious but useless.—CAMPBELL'S CHIEF JUSTICES.

Sir William Temple.—He is not without pretensions to the most honorable place among the statesmen of his time. Yet Temple is not a man to our taste. A temper not naturally good, but under strict command,—a constant regard to decorum, a rare caution in playing that mixed game of skill and hazard, human life; a disposition to be content with small but certain winnings rather than go on doubling the stake,—these seem to us to be the most remarkable features of his character. This sort of moderation when united, as in him it was, with very considerable abilities, is, under ordinary circumstances, scarcely to be distinguished from the highest and purest integrity ; and yet may be perfectly compatible with laxity of principle, with coldness of heart, and with the most intense selfishness. Temple, we fear, had not sufficient warmth and elevation of sentiment to deserve the name of a virtuous man. He did not betray or oppress his country: nay, he rendered considerable service to her, but he did nothing for her. No temptation which either the king or the opposition could hold out ever induced him to come forward as the supporter either of arbitrary or of factious measures. But he was most careful never to give offence by strenuously opposing such measures. He never put himself prominently before the public eye, except at conjunctures when he was almost certain to gain, and could not possibly lose ;—at conjunctures when the interest of the state, the views of the court, and the passions of the multitude all appeared for an instant to coincide. By judiciously availing himself of several of these rare moments, he succeeded in establishing a high character for wisdom and patriotism. When the favorable crisis was passed, he never risked a reputation which he had won. He avoided the great offices of state with a caution almost pusillanimous, and confined himself to quiet and secluded departments of public business, in which he could enjoy moderate but certain advantage without incurring envy. If the circumstances of the country became such that it was impossible to take any part in politics without some danger, he retired to his library and his orchard; and, while the nation groaned under oppression, or resounded with tumult and with the din of civil arms, amused himself by writing memoirs and tying up apricots. Of course a man is not bound to be a politician any more than he is bound to be a soldier; and there are perfectly honorable ways of quitting both politics and the military profession. But neither in the one way of life, nor in the other, is any man entitled to take all the sweet and leave all the sour. A man who belongs to the army only in time of peace,—who appears at reviews in Hyde Park, escorts the sovereign with the utmost valor and fidelity to and from the House of Lords, and retires as soon as he thinks it likely that he may be ordered on an expedition—is justly thought to have disgraced himself. Some portion of a censure due to such a holiday-soldier may justly fall on the mere holiday-politician, who flinches from his duties as soon as those duties become difficult and disagreeable;—that is to say, as soon as it becomes peculiarly important that he should resolutely perform them.

He loved fame, but not with the love of an exalted and generous mind. He loved it as an end, not at all as a means;—as a personal luxury, not at all as an instrument of advantage to others. He scraped it together and treasured it up with a timid and niggardly thrift, and never employed the hoard in any enterprise, however virtuous and honorable, in which there was hazard of losing one particle. It was his constitution to dread failure more than he desired success,—to prefer security, comfort, repose, leisure, to the turmoil and anxiety which are inseparable from greatness; and this natural languor of mind when contrasted with the malignant energy of the keen and restless spirits among whom his lot was cast, sometimes appears to resemble the moderation of virtue. But we must own that he seems to us to sink into littleness and meanness when we compare him—we do not say with any high standard of morality,—but with many of those frail men who, aiming at noble· ends, but often drawn from the right path by strong passions and strong temptations, have left to posterity a doubtful and checkered fame.—MACAULAY.

25. *Let every man abide in the same calling wherein he was called.*

Probably, I should not consciously and deliberately forsake my particular calling to do the good which society demands of me, to save the universe from annihilation; and I believe that a like, but infinitely greater steadfastness elsewhere is all that preserves it.—THOREAU.

A man may contribute his share to the welfare of society, by inspiring his time with a better knowledge of things, which knowledge is to elevate the masses of men.—BEECHER.

This is a place to give a man chances, and try what stuff is in him. The office involves a talent for governing as well as for judging ; talent for fighting also, in cases of extremity, and what is still better a talent for avoiding to fight.—CARLYLE.

To his own master he standeth or falleth.

Finite reason standing alone in its own individuality, has its own peculiar measure, and so its self-insight has its peculiar clearness, compass, and systematic consistency, and so, too, each finite intelligence has knowledge peculiarly its own, and not another's, and wherein the knowing is relative to himself, and not properly universal.—HICKOK.

I am of the opinion that every mind that comes into the world has its own specialty—is different from every other mind ; and that every young man and every young woman is a failure so long as each does not find what is his or her own bias ; that just so long as you are influenced by those around you, so long as you are attempting to do those things which you see others do well, instead of doing that thing which you can do well, you are so far wrong, so far failing of your own right mark. . . Though one may easily be mistaken for a time, yet there is in his mind this particular fitness for a calling ; and some things that he can do, as in mathematics, or in right arrangements of facts ; he being able to distribute the duties of the day ; the distribution of facts in his mind, so that he understands and can recite history better than any other ; or the perception of his aim, and keeping that through all the particulars by which a logical mind acts, in various ways, as some eyes are made for color and some for form. —EMERSON.

There are problematic characters who are not equal to any situation in life, and whom no situation satisfies. This causes an immense discord within, and their whole life is spent without enjoyment.— GOETHE.

> ' No, let them feel that their lame are strong—
>   That their courage will fail them never,
> Who strike to repay long years of wrong,
>   And bury past shame forever.'

For if the trumpet give an uncertain sound who shall prepare himself to the battle.

Difficulty and toil give the soul strength to crush in a loftier region the passions which draw strength only from earth. So long as we listen to the purer promptings within us, there is a power invisible, though not unfelt which protects us. Amid the toil of tumult, and soiling struggle, there is ever an eye that watches, ever a heart that overflows with Infinite and Almighty Love.—BAYARD TAYLOR.

Self-conquest involves more than the subjugation of the body. The mind itself must be under control. True Christian manhood includes the power to govern the temper, the imagination, the memory, the taste, the affections. It includes the power of application, of abstraction : the power to direct the course of one's thoughts; and to resist ignoble mental impulses.

27. *Tasks.*—Remember that work consolidates, that it puts the needed restrictions, favors revolving and essential possession : that there is nothing that so compacts and fastens, makes own our meditations and attainments, as this agency. If he have, as many may, legitimate ulterior tasks and labors, in whose performance he delights, and to which he looks as his proper life-work, let him keep his eye fixed, refusing to forget himself, or become absorbed or preoccupied in the subordinate and relative.

Let there be review and improvement; all the work carefully laid out; not too much undertaken; not too little accepted. There is recognition that we are in the midst of temptation, exposure. All the agencies may be invoked for arming; everything that can contribute to lift and to hold.

Man's destiny and function is to do and he decays, grows to mere sentimentalism and sickly effeminacy, if he apply not his strength to work and the homeliest tasks.—MILLS.

Heroism is very homely work in the doing, and immortal deeds look prosaic and fool-hardy to the mole-eyed worldly wisdom of to-day.—RICHARDSON.

28. It has been observed, that men of learning who take to business discharge it generally with

greater honesty than men of the world. The chief reason for it, I take to be, as follows: A man that has spent his youth in reading, has been used to find virtue extolled, and vice stigmatized. A man that has passed his time in the world, has often seen vice triumphant, and virtue discountenanced. Extortion, rapine, and injustice, which are branded with infamy in books, often give a man a figure in the world; while several good qualities which are celebrated in authors, as generosity, ingenuity, and good nature, impoverish and ruin him. This cannot but have a proportionable effect on men whose tempers and principles are equally good and vicious.—ADDISON.

A good tree can not bring forth evil fruit.

Walter Scott's father.—My father was a singular instance of a man's rising to eminence in a profession for which nature had in some degree unfitted him. He had, indeed, a turn for labor, and a pleasure in analyzing the abstruse feudal doctrines of conveyancing, which would probably have rendered him unrivalled in the line of a special pleader, had there been such a profession in Scotland; but in the actual business of the profession which he embraced, in that sharpened intuitive perception which is necessary in driving bargains for himself and others, in·availing himself of the wants, necessities, caprices, and follies of some, and guarding against the knaving and malice of others, uncle Toby himself could not have conducted himself with more simplicity than my father.

Most attorneys have been suspected more or less justly of making their own fortune at the expense of their clients: my father's fate was to vindicate his calling from the stain in one instance, for in many cases his clients contrived to ease him of considerable sums. Many worshipful and benighted names recur to my memory who did him the honor to run him in debt to the amount of thousands, and to pay him with a law-suit or a commission of bankruptcy, as the case happened. But they are gone to a different accounting, and it would be ungenerous to visit their disgrace upon their descendants. He had a zeal for his clients which was almost ludicrous: far from coldly discharging the duties of his employment toward them, he thought for them, felt for their honor, as for his own, and rather risked disobliging them than neglecting anything to which he conceived their duty bound them. If there was any old mother or aunt to be maintained, he was, I am afraid, too apt to administer to their necessities from what the young heir had destined his own pleasures.

Chief Justice Holt.— From his start as a magistrate, he exceeded the high expectations which had been formed of him, and during the long period of twenty-two years, he constantly rose in the admiration and esteem of his countrymen. To unsullied integrity and lofty independence, he added a rare combination of deep professional knowledge with exquisite common sense. According to a homely but expressive phrase—'there was no rubbish in his mind.' Familiar with the practice of the court as any clerk, acquainted with the rules of special pleading as if he had spent all his days and nights in drawing declarations and demurrers, versed in the subtleties of the law of real property, as if he had confined his attention to conveyancing, and as a commercial lawyer much in advance of any of his contemporaries—he ever reasoned logically—appearing at the same time instinctively acquainted with all the feelings of the human heart, and versed by experience in all the ways of mankind. He may be considered as having a genius for magistracy as much as our Milton had for poetry, or our Wilkie for painting. Perhaps the excellence which he attained may be traced to the passion for justice by which he was constantly actuated. This induced him to sacrifice ease, and amusement and literary relaxation, and the allurements of party, to submit to tasks the most dull, disagreeable, and revolting, and to devote all his energies to one object, ever ready to exclaim—

> Welcome business, welcome strife,
> Welcome the cares of ermined life,
> The visage wan, the purblind sight,
> The toil by day, the lamp by night,
> The tedious forms, the solemn prate,
> The pert dispute, the dull debate,
> The drowsy bench, the babbling hall,
> For thee, fair Justice, welcome all!

'The criminal before him knew that, though his spirit was broken with guilt, and incapable of language to defend itself, his judge would wrest no law to destroy him, nor conceal any that would save him. He never spared vice, at the same time he could see through the hypocrisy and disguise of those who have no pretence to virtue themselves, but by their severity to the vicious.—TATLER.

During a century and a half this country has been renowned above all others, for the pure and enlightened administration of justice: and Holt is the model on which, in England, the judicial character has been formed.—CAMPBELL.

Coke.—He had a passionate attachment to his own calling—thus he addresses the young beginner:—For thy encouragement, cast thine eyes upon the sages of the law that have been before thee, and never shalt thou find any that hath excelled in the knowledge of the laws, but hath sucked from the breasts of that divine knowledge, honesty, gravity, and integrity, and by the goodness of God hath obtained a greater blessing than any other profession to their family and posterity.—CAMPBELL.

29. *The physician.*—No class of men in the regular discharge of duty incur danger more frequently than the honest physician. There is no type of malignant maladies with which he fails to become acquainted; no hospital so crowded with contagion that he dares not walk freely through its wards. His

11*

vocation is among the sick and dying ; he is the familiar friend of those who are sinking under infectious disease ; he never shrinks from the horror of observing it under all aspects. He must do so with equanimity ; as he inhales the poisoned atmosphere, he must coolly reflect on the medicines which may mitigate the sufferings that he cannot remedy. Nay, after death has ensued, he must search with the dissecting knife for its hidden cause, if so by multiplying his own perils, he may discover some alleviation for the affliction of others. And why is this? Because the physician is indifferent to death? Because he is steeled and hardened against the fear of it? By no means. It is his especial business to value life ; to cherish the spark of animated existence. And the habit of caring for lives of his fellow-men is far from leading him to habitual indifference to his own. The physician shuns every danger but such as the glory of his profession commands him to defy.'

No science has such extensive and intimate connections with other sciences. It gathers to itself the resources of chemistry, botany, mechanics, comparative anatomy, and physiology, and mental philosophy ; and fills its storehouse of facts with a variety and abundance sufficient to satisfy the wildest and most eager curiosity. The phenomena of life even in the healthy condition are exceedingly diversified ; but as modified by disease, and by the remedies which are administered, their variations

are never ending. And then the mysterious connection of mind and body not only varies them still
more, but opens to us a mass of facts of a mingled
mental and physical character, which awaken an intense interest. The physician looks upon the human
body, not merely as a machine filled with contrivan-
ces so cunning and elaborate as to render all the
mechanism of man in the comparison rude and
bungling: but as a machine instinct with life, having a living nerve attached to every fibre of it.

The details of a science which treats of phenomena
so interesting in their character, and so wide in their
range, are never dry and uninteresting, as the details
of other sciences sometimes are. There are no tedi-
ous technicalities, no dull abstractions—no tiresome
monotony. There is, therefore, an absorbing enthusiasm in the pursuit of medical science, which
makes its votary disregard the loathsomeness of pu-
trefaction and even forget danger in his search after
truth.—HOOKER.

9. *Greeley.*—His very name a title-page, and next
His life a commentary on the text.—WOODBRIDGE.

My life has been busy and anxious, but not joyless.
Whether it shall be prolonged few or more years, I
am grateful that it has endured so long, and that it
has abounded in opportunities for good not wholly
unimproved, and in experiences of the nobler as well
as the baser impulses of human nature. I have
been spared to see the end of giant wrongs, which I

once deemed invincible in this century, and to note the silent upspringing and growth of principles and influences which I hail as destined to root out some of the most flagrant and pervading evils that yet remain. I realize that each generation is destined to confront new and peculiar trials—to wrestle with temptations and seductions unknown to its predecessors : yet I trust that progress is a general law of our being, and that the ills and woes of the future shall be less crushing than those of the bloody and hateful past. So, looking calmly, yet humbly, for that close of my mortal career which cannot be far distant, I reverently thank God for the blessings vouchsafed me in the past, and with an awe that is not fear, and a consciousness of demerit which does not exclude hope, await the opening before my steps of the gates of the eternal world.—GREELEY.

Before the burial.—Now, now, we measure at its worth
The gracious presence gone forever !
The wrinkled East that gave him birth,
Laments with every laboring river;
Wild moan the free winds of the West
For him who gathered to her prairies
The sons of men, and made each crest
The haunt of happy household fairies.

The tears that fall from eyes unused,—
The hands above his grave united,—
The words of men whose lips he loosed,
Whose cross he bore, whose wrongs he righted,—
Could he but know, and rest with this !

Yet, stay through Death's low-lying hollow,
His one last foe's insatiate hiss
On that benignant shade would follow !
—STEDMAN.

Prentice to Greeley.—
But thou hast well fufilled thy trust,
Still foremost mid thy fellow-men,
Though in each year of all thy time,
Thou hast compressed three-score and ten ;—
For I have marked thy strong career
As traced by thy own sturdy pen.

In this one man is shown a temperance, proof
Against all trials : industry severe
And constant as the motion of the day :
Stern self-denial round him spread, with shade
That might be deemed forbidding, did not there
All generous feelings flourish and rejoice.
—WORDSWORTH.]

This concord of a well-tuned mind
Hath been so set by that all-working hand
Of heaven, that though the world done its worst
To put it out by discords most unkind :
Yet doth it still in perfect union stand
With God and man.—DANIEL.

10. *Labor—Ye said also, Behold what a weariness is it!*

Calvin.—What shall I say of his indefatigable industry, almost beyond the power of nature, which paralleled with our loiterings, will, I fear, exceed all credit ? It may be the truest object of admiration,

how one lean, worn, spent, and wearied body could
hold out. He read, every week of the year through,
three divinity-lectures; every other week, over and
above he preached every day; so that, (as Erasmus
said of Chrysostom) I know not whether more to
admire his constancy, or theirs that heard him. Some
have reckoned his yearly lectures to be 186, and his
yearly sermons 286. Every Thursday he sat in the
presbytery; every Friday when the ministers met to
consult upon difficult texts, he made as good as a lec-
ture. Besides all this, there was scarce a day that
exercised him not in answering either by word of
mouth or writing, the doubts and questions of different
churches and pastors; yea, sometimes more than
once: so that he might say with Paul, 'The care of all
churches lieth upon me:' scarcely a year wherein,
over and above all these employments, some great
volume in folio came not forth.'—Hoyt.

'I saw Italy only to leave it,' said Calvin with a
sigh. Returning to France he sold the property
which he had inherited from his father—and set out
for Strasburg. Yet not without regret did he leave
his native France. 'Every step toward the border
costs me tears,' he said, 'yet, if the truth cannot dwell
in France, I will not.' . . Calvin at once gave
himself to the work of making Geneva a Christian
city. The rigor with which he assailed the customs
of a pleasure-loving people awakened at length a
growing opposition, and in 1538 he was banished

from the city. Near the close of the year 1540, the authorities of Geneva besought Calvin to return to their city. The years of his absence—years of tumult and disorder in Geneva—had borne witness to the value of his presence and teaching. Calvin was now firmly established in Strasburg. He had married there also, and had little desire moreover, to mingle again in the stormy scenes which he had witnessed in Geneva. Yet, he could not refuse the call; and he set out for Geneva saying : 'I bring my bleeding heart a sacrifice to the Lord.' People came forth in crowds to meet him : before his death, in 1564, such a change had been wrought in that once gay and thoughtless city that Farel, pointing to Geneva, could say : 'There the pure Gospel is preached in all temples and houses : there the music of psalms never ceases : there hands are folded and hearts are lifted up to heaven from morning till night ! '—BURRAGE.

Robertson at Oxford.—His friends were sought among the thinking, the literary, the devout-minded, and intellectual men of his day. Light and trivial, or foolish conversation was always most abhorrent to him. His idea and endeavor with respect to social enjoyment were mental gain or spiritual improvement.

Mere recreation or mere amusement were regarded by him as little better than waste of time. The common every-day talk, the joke, the sharp repartee of men fresh from public schools and elated with youthful spirits, found no sympathy in his breast, and were positively distasteful to him. He would often say with emphasis : ' To think that men should have nothing better to converse about than all this trash ! ' His turn of mind led him to an almost contemptuous dislike for what he called ' the froth, the scum, the vanity of all these things ! '—CLARKE.

Robertson at Brighton.—' I cannot describe to you in words the strange sensation, during his sermon, of union with him and communion with one another which filled us as he spoke. Nor can I describe to you the sense we had of a higher Presence,—the sacred awe which filled our hearts,—the hushed stillness in which the smallest sound was startling,—the calmed eagerness of men who listened as if waiting for a word of revelation to resolve the doubt or to heal the sorrow of a life,—the unexpected light which came upon the faces of some when an expression struck home and made them feel,—in a moment of high relief from pain or doubt,—this man speaks to *me*, and his words are inspired by God. And when the close came, and silence almost awful fell upon the church, even after a sigh of relief from strained attention had ceased to come from all the congregation, I have often seen men so wrapt that they could not move till the sound of the organ aroused them to the certainty that the preacher had ceased to speak.' ⸴

Judson.—No description could convey the peculiar impression of his manner,—so quiet, so simple and humble, yet breathing a hush, a thrill through the assembly, such as I have never witnessed elsewhere. We felt that we were in the presence of one who had 'entered within the vail,' one conversant beyond most of his fellow-men with the mysteries of the invisible world, and whose life was 'hid with Christ in God.'—MRS. CONANT.

For the priest's lips should keep knowledge, and they should seek the law at his mouth: for he is the messenger of the Lord of hosts.

10. *The Prophet.*—*The Lord God will raise up unto thee a Prophet from the midst of thee, of thy brethren.*

Prophecy.—'Gift of insight.'—'Power of explaining truth.'—'A declaration of the divine prescience, looking at any distance through a train of infinite causes known and unknown to us, upon a sure and certain effect.'

A Revelation to be satisfactory, must be complete, harmonious in itself, and addressed to the world through living teachers.—INDEPENDENT.

The prophetic state :—The bodily senses were closed to external objects as in deep sleep. The reflective and discursive faculty was still and inactive. The spiritual faculty was awakened to the highest state of energy. Hence it is, that revelations in trances are described by the prophets as 'seen' or 'heard' by them; for the spiritual faculty energizes by immediate perception on the part of the inward sense, not by inference and thought.—SMITH.

> ' While watching on our arms at night,
> We heard thy call, we felt thy light.—'

*And I turned to see the voice that spake with me—
like unto the son of man.*

*I, John, who am also your brother and companion
in tribulation.*

For in the case of every prophet, the divine element in him comes into contact with sin in his contemporaries, and the closer their relation in the flesh,
the more incomprehensible to the worldly man is
their wide separation in the spirit. The spectacle of
the prophet entangled in the same irritating cares of
daily life, that are common to all his fellows, rendered
it more difficult under this lowly guise to recognize
his heavenly character.—OLSHAUSEN.

*Moses.—With him will I speak mouth to mouth—
and the similitude of the Lord shall he behold.*

When we see him at the Burning Bush sacrificing
his diffidence to his duty, and resolving finally to
attempt the first great liberation of mankind ;—when
we trace him through the wonders of Sinai, and of
the wilderness, when we mark his steady faith in
God, his undoubting obedience to every divine command ; his unexampled patriotism, immovable by
ingratitude, rebellion, and insult ; his cheerful communication of every office of power and profit to
others, and his equally cheerful exclusion of his own
descendants from all places of distinction ; when we
consider his glorious integrity in adhering always to

the duties of his office, unseduced by power and splendor, unmoved by national and singular homage, unawed by faction and opposition, undaunted by danger and difficulty, and unaltered by provocation, obloquy, and distress; when we see him meek beyond example, and patient and persevering through forty years of declining life, in toil, hazard, and trial; when we read in his writings the frank records of his own failings and that of his family, friends, and nation, and the first efforts of the historian, the poet, the orator, and the lawgiver; when we see all the duties of self-government, benevolence, and piety, which he taught exactly displayed in a life approximating to angelic virtue; when we behold him the deliverer of his nation, the restorer of truth, the pillar of righteousness, and the reformer of mankind : his whole character shines with a radiance like the splendor which his face derived from the Son of Righteousness, and on which the human eye could not endure to look. He is everywhere the same glorious person; the man of God, selected from the race of Adam, called up into the mountain that burned with fire; ascending to meet his Creator; embosoming himself in the clouds of Sinai; walking calmly onward through the thunders and lightnings; and serenely advancing to the immediate presence and converse of Jehovah. He is the greatest of all prophets; the first type of the Saviour, conducted to Pisgah, unclothed of mortal flesh and entombed in the dust by the immediate hand of the Most High.—DWIGHT.

11. *The perfect historian* is he in whose work the character and spirit of an age is exhibited in miniature. He relates no fact, he attributes no expression to his characters, which is not authenticated by sufficient testimony. But by judicious selection, rejection, and arrangement, he gives to truth those attractions which have been usurped by fiction. In his narrative a due subordination is observed ; some transactions are prominent, others retire. But the scale on which he represents them is increased or diminished, not according to the dignity of the persons concerned in them, but according to the degree in which they elucidate the condition of society and the nature of man. He considers no anecdote, no peculiarity of mind, no familiar saying as too insignificant for his notice, which is not too insignificant to illustrate the operation of laws, of religion, and of education, and to mark the progress of the human mind. Men will not merely be described, but will be made intimately known to us.—MACAULAY.

History with faithful Genius at the top, and faithful Industry at the bottom will then be capable of being written. History will then actually be written— the inspired gift of God—employing itself to illuminate the dark ways of God—a thing pressingly needful to be done, whereby modern nations may again become a little less godless, and again have several things they are still more fatally in want of at present.—CARLYLE.

12. *The dark ages.*—

> Strange, salty odors through the darkness steal,
> And through the dark the ocean thunders roll;
> Thick darkness gathers stifling, till I feel
> > Its weight upon my soul.
> I strain my eyes into the heavy night—
> Blackness of Darkness!'

Christianity entered into the race and the individual as a new life—a regeneration—awakening new principles of action, new motives and affections, creating aspirations after holiness-for its own sake.— BLAKE.

At the close of the third century after Christ, the prospects of mankind were fearfully dreary. Philosophy remained stationary.

A (Roman) sovereign almost invisible; a crowd of dignitaries minutely distinguished by badges and titles; rhetoricians who said nothing but what had been said ten thousand times; schools in which nothing was taught but what had been known for ages —such was the machinery provided for the government and instruction of the most enlightened part of the human race. That great community was then in danger of experiencing a calamity far more terrible than any of the quick, inflammatory, destroying maladies, to which nations are liable—a tottering, drivelling, paralytic longevity, the immortality of the Struldbrugs, a Chinese civilization.

From this miserable state the Western Empire was saved by the fiercest and most destroying visitation with which God has ever chastened his creatures—the invasion of the northern nations. Such a cure was required for such a distemper. The fire of London, it has been observed, was a blessing. It burned down the city, but it burned out the plague. The same may be said of the tremendous devastation of the Roman dominions. It annihilated the noisome recesses in which lurked the seeds of great moral maladies; it cleared an atmosphere fatal to the health and vigor of the human mind. It cost Europe a thousand years of barbarism to escape the fate of China. At length, the terrible purification was accomplished; and the second civilization of mankind commenced, under circumstances which afforded a strong security that it would never retrograde and never pause.—MACAULAY.

Retrogressions of the human intellect.—It is curious that in the most disturbed period of this turbulent reign (King Henry III.), when ignorance seemed to be thickening and the human intellect to decline, there was written and given to the world the best treatise upon law of which England could boast till the publication of Blackstone's Commentaries in the middle of the eighteenth century. For comprehensiveness, for lucid arrangement, for logical precision, this author (Bracton) was unrivalled during many ages.—CAMPBELL.

There is no part of English history since the Conquest, so uncertain, so little authentic or consistent, as that of the wars between the two Roses: and it is remarkable that this profound darkness falls upon us just on the eve of the restoration of letters, and when the art of printing was already known in Europe. All that we can distinguish with certainty through the deep cloud which covers that period, is a scene of horror and bloodshed, savage manners, arbitrary executions, and treacherous, dishonorable conduct in all parties.—HUME.

Revolutions.—Periods of Revolution bring out and develop extraordinary characters; they produce saints and heroes, and they produce also fanatics and fools and villains; but they are unfavorable to the action of average conscientious men, and to the application of· the plain principles of right and wrong to every-day life. Common men at such times see all things changing round them,—institutions falling to ruin; religious truth no longer an awful and undisputed reality, but an opinion shifting from hour to hour; and they are apt to think that, after all, interest is the best object for which to live, and that in the general scramble those are the wisest who best take care of themselves.

Meanwhile, a vast intellectual revolution, of which the religious reformation was rather a sign than a cause, was making its way in the English mind. The discovery of the form of the earth and of its place in the planetary system was producing an effect on the imagination which long familiarity with the truth renders it hard for us now to realize. The very heaven itself had been rolled up like a scroll, laying bare the illimitable abyss of space; the solid frame of the earth had become a transparent ball, and in a hemisphere below their feet, men saw the sunny Palm Isles and the golden glories of the tropic seas. Long impassive, long unable from the very toughness of their natures to apprehend these novel wonders, indifferent to them, even hating them as at first they hated the doctrines of Luther, the English opened their eyes at last. In the convulsions which rent England from the Papacy, a thousand superstitions were blown away; a thousand new thoughts rushed in, bringing with them their train of new desires and new emotions: and when the fire was once kindled, the dry wood burnt fiercely in the wind.—FROUDE.

Gen. Monk and the Restoration.—Revolutions leave so much distrust and distaste for violent proceedings in the minds of all men of sense who have gone through them, that they feel a repugnance to have recourse to them themselves, even when their employment seems easy and their success assured.

The more important the step which Monk had taken, the more determined was he to do nothing precipitately, and to go no further until the propitious moment arrived when he could act under the pressure of necessity, and with the appearance of legality. His good sense and practical experience had taught him that; in order to exert a powerful influence over men, whether friends or enemies, it is necessary to act in the name of some acknowledged right, some undisputed principle, which may serve as a starting-point and standard in action. He had now found, or to speak more correctly, events had supplied him with the support so necessary to his first steps on the difficult course on which he had entered. He had now a legitimate right to use the cloak with which he had hitherto covered his real purpose; his acts were sanctioned by the last surviving representatives of that Old Parliament whose servant he professed himself to be.

On the very day after the Restoration the court and the puritans were the two hostile forces which appeared at the two opposite extremities of the political arena.

The period of civil war was passed; that of parliamentary conflicts and compromises was beginning. The sway of Protestant religion and the decisive influence of the country in its own government— these were the objects which Revolutionary England had pursued. Though cursing the revolution and calling it the rebellion, Royalist England nevertheless prepared still to pursue these objects, and not to rest till she had attained them.—GUIZOT.

English liberty had been the slow fruit of ages, still waiting a happier season for its perfect ripeness, but already giving proof of the vigor and

industry which had been employed in its culture.—
HALLAM.

13. *The Divine Counsels.*—*He causeth it to come,*
whether for correction, or for his land, or for mercy.
And it is turned round about by his counsels, that he
may do whatever he commandeth them.

' Every now and then, God brings the human race
to a crisis. The times become grand and solemn.
The soul of the race seems to vibrate to its remotest
extremities.'

Kings are lifted up or thrown down; nations come
and go; republics flourish and wither; dynasties
pass away like a tale that is told; but nothing is by
chance, though men in their ignorance of causes may
think so. The caprice of fleeting existences bends
to the immovable omnipotence which has neither
change of purpose nor repose. Sometimes like a
messenger through the thick darkness of night, it
steps along mysterious ways, but when the hour
strikes for a people or for mankind to pass into a
new form of being, unseen hands draw the bolts from
the gates of futurity; an all-subduing influence prepares the mind of men for the coming revolution:
those who plan resistance find themselves in conflict
with the will of Providence rather than with human
devices; and all hearts and all understandings, most
of all the opinions and influences of the unwilling
are wonderfully attracted and compelled to bear forward the change which becomes more an obedience

to the law of universal nature, than submission to the arbitrament of man.—BANCROFT.

How long shall it be to the end of these wonders?

God's kingdom in this world goes on secretly and silently and hiddenly, both in the individual and the community; and is often disclosed as a thing accomplished, long after men have given over hope and expectation.—BEECHER.

The race has entered on the period when its previous education has ripened, and truth begins to bring forth her perfect fruits. . . Having thus traced man's progress from unconsciousness to instinct, from instinct to discipline, from discipline to faith and liberty, the inquiry naturally arises, whether in these, so far as they shall be manifested or experienced on earth, the race will find its last stage of advancement? To this question, that great eternal future which shall open to all of us, can alone supply the full response. Yet as to the nature of that response, revelation offers no indistinct intimations.—BLAKE.

17. *Where there is no vision the people perish.*

When truth ceases to go out of us as action, it will soon cease to come in to us as vision. The greatest souls of history have not been those to whom the finest visions were vouchsafed : but those who have not disobeyed the visions they have beheld while others slept the sleep of sense and sin. And the great nation is not of necessity the nation that has embodied them in her customs, processes, and laws.—CHADWICK.

Present Apostasy.—Because my people hath forgotten me, they have burned incense to vanity and they have caused them to stumble in their ways from the ancient paths.—

There are none of us willing to admit that the human race is going backward, and yet we cannot deny that there are great counter-currents of evil, which sometimes seem to check the moral progress of a people. Such an one seems flowing out from the war.—M. C. A.

The forty-second Congress will be chiefly remembered for scandalous exposures which have not been followed by purification; delinquencies of members which have not been punished; and the discovery of abuses in the public service without a consequent reformation.—TRIBUNE.

For every one from the least even unto the greatest is given to covetousness.

*Reforms.—*It is a curious illustration of the existing condition of society that the principal difficulties of reform conventions should be in finding thrust upon them as candidates men who are in reality necessarily opposed to all their plans. Indeed, these reform commotions, both in the prodigious heat and energy displayed at first, and the extreme ignorance and gullibility exhibited in the later stages, have rather an Asiatic than an American look, and sometimes

has seen the most majestic visions of the right
and true, but the nation which having seen them
make one think that the world may be slowly working its way back ' down the ringing grooves' of Progress to that condition of society in which reform
movements consist of alternate advances, devasta-
tions, and retreats of vast hordes of semi-barbarous
men under the leadership of powerful chieftains
who live partly on the plunder of the enemy and
partly on that of their subjects.—NATION.

*For among my people are found wicked men:—they
set a trap, they catch men.*

*They are waxen fat, they shine:—they judge not the
cause, the cause of the fatherless, yet they prosper;
and the right of the needy do they not judge. Shall I
not visit for these things? saith the Lord.*

> The God who with his finger drew
> The judgment coming on,—
> Write for these men what must ensue
> Ere many years be gone!—DICKENS.

20. *National Judgments.*—
> 'Tremendous judgments from thy hand
> Thy dreadful power display.'

*Extracts from the Evening Post's summary of the
year.*—Jan. 4. Violent and unusual shocks of earthquake in England.

1–8. In Philadelphia 230 persons die of small-pox.

12. Small-pox spreads in all parts of England,
Scotland, and Ireland.

19. Great earthquake at Shemache, Causas; 137 killed, 44 wounded, and te hcity ruined.

26. Terrible floods in England, with immense loss of property.

Feb. 4. Remarkable aurora witnessed in America, Europe, Asia, and the southern hemisphere.

19. A Boston paper of to-day reports 27 persons frozen to death, 34 cases of crime, and an earthquake.

March 26. Dreadful earthquake in California; 1,500 miles of country shaken; 40 people killed, 100 wounded. Seven thousand shocks were felt in three days.

27. Destructive earthquake at Oaxaca, Mexico.

Apr. 3. Antioch destroyed by a great earthquake that caused the death of two thousand persons; ten thousand houses burnt at Jeddo.

5. Ten tons of obscene literature seized in New York.

16. An earthquake at Memphis.

25–27. Grand eruption of Vesuvius and loss of two hundred lives. The most terrible for two centuries.

28. Strike of two thousand cartmen at Liverpool.

May 11. Riot and strike of fifteen hundred miners in Michigan.

12. The great strikes in New York and Brooklyn begin.

June 19. It is reported that a strange plague in

three towns in Brazil had destroyed eight thousand people out of a population of thirteen thousand.

20. Twenty thousand miners on a strike in Germany.

21. Revolution in Peru with fearful carnage.

28. Huge sun spots seen many days.

August 14. Great heat and awful convulsions of the atmosphere.

15. Great riots in Belfast, Ireland.

17. A three weeks' strike of shoe-makers ends at Lynn.

29. Cholera in India and West Russia.

Sep. 9. Fifteen or twenty thousand Indians on the war path in Yellowstone·Valley.

17. New and fatal cattle plague in Nevada.

18. Defalcation of $180,000 in the United States Treasury in New York.

24. Great Britain suffering from coal famine, great rains, potato-rot and poor harvests.

29. Great gales, and *immense* losses in the western lakes.

Oct. 1. The strange horse epizoötic begins in Ontario—in two months time attacks nearly five million horses.

2. The famous Escurial in Spain struck by lightning and damaged $200,000.

5. Spain sends fourteen thousand more troops to Cuba.

10. It is announced in Persia that three million persons have died of famine and plague.

Nov. 9–10. Terrible conflagration in Boston. Loss about $100,000,000

18. In Russia eighty thousand people have died up to this time of cholera.

3. Gas stokers strike in London.

17. Awful storms and floods in France and England.

> ' Vast magazines of plagues and storms
> Lie treasured for his foes.'

If that nation against whom I have pronounced evil turn from their evil, I will repent. of the evil I thought to do unto them.

> ' No more the sovereign eye of God
> O'erlooks the crimes of men.'

25th December!—Silently the month advances. There is nothing to destroy but much to bury. Bury, then, thou snow, that slumberously fallest through the still air, the hedge-rows of leaves! Muffle thy cold wool about the feet of shivering trees! Bury all that the year hath known, and let thy brilliant stars, that never shine as they do in thy frostiest nights, behold the work! But know, O month of destruction, that in thy constellation is set that Star whose rising is the sign, forevermore, that there is life in death! Thou art the month of Resurrection. In thee, the Christ came. Every star that looks upon thy labor and toil of burial, knows that all things shall come forth again. Storms shall sob themselves to sleep. Silence shall find a voice. Death shall live, Life shall rejoice.—BEECHER.

And it came to pass on a certain day as he was teaching, that there were Pharisees and doctors of the law sitting by which were come out of every town of Galilee and Judea and Jerusalem : and the power of the Lord was present to heal them.

The sea of Galilee has no sacred associations but those of the New Testament. One peaceful presence dwells undisturbed on its shores and its waters from end to end.

It was still winter or early spring : four months yet to the harvest, and the bright, golden ears of those fields had not yet whitened their golden expanse of verdure. But at he gazed upon them, they served to present the glorious vision of the distant harvest of the Gentile world, which with each successive turn of the conversation unfolded itself more distinctly before him as he sate absorbed in the opening prospect,—silent amid his silent and astonished disciples.—STANLEY.

Ask for me and I will give thee the heathen for thine inheritance, and the uttermost part of the earth for thy possession.

> ' See a long race thy spacious courts adorn,
> See future sons and daughters yet unborn,
> In crowding ranks on every side arise
> Demanding life, impatient for the skies.
> See barbarous nations at thy gate attend,

12*

Walk in thy light and in thy temple bend:
See thy bright altars thronged with prostrate kings,
While every land its joyous tribute brings.'

Christ speaks, and at once generations become his by stricter, closer ties than those of blood—by the most sacred, most indissoluble of all unions. He lights up the flame of love which consumes self-love, which prevails over every other love. In this wonderful power of his will we recognize the Word that created the world.—NAPOLEON.

He tasted death for every man.

An eternal glory has been shed upon the human race by the love Christ bore to it. And as love provokes love, many have found it possible to conceive for Christ an attachment the closeness of which no words can describe, a veneration so possessing and absorbing the man within them, that they have said, ' I live no more, but Christ lives in me.' Now such a feeling carries with it of necessity the feeling of love for all human beings. It matters no longer what quality men may exhibit, amiable or unamiable, as the brothers of Christ, as belonging to His sacred and consecrated kind, as the objects of His love in life and death, they must be dear to all to whom He is dear. And those who would for a moment know His heart and understand His life, must begin with thinking of the whole race with awful reverence and hope.—ECCE HOMO.

27. *Confidence in Truth.*—Christ believed that His

mission was of God, the purpose which he was un-
folding and executing was God's ; and the infinite
resources of God were pledged to its realization.
He looked to that universal providence which includes mind as well as matter, and to its mighty
combinations and agencies. He looked to the overflowing and inexhaustible fountain of spiritual influences, and his confidence was untroubled and sérene.
—YOUNG.

How little and mean is the confidence of man in
God!—LUTHER.

The plain fact is, that confidence in truth is not a
common thing in the world, even in the nominally
Christian world. He who loves the truth will of
course defend it in his turn—will fight for it, and be
spit upon for it, and if need be, die for it, being very
zealous for its honor, and ambitious for its triumphs:
but he will not distrust it. Like Luther, he will take
heart by looking up to the unsupported skies—seeing
God where no visible secrets are. He will confide
in the truth because it is of God ; and will as soon
expect the stars to fall, as the heavenly arch of truth.
And there are two streams that flow to fill the channel
of his faith ; one out of the nature of truth itself, and
the other out of the fields of history. Reposing on this
ennobling trust, he will valiantly believe that error,
though built into broad-based and solid pyramids,
will crumble to the dust under the feet of marching
centuries, and that truth though it be burned in the

hottest flames, will, like the phœnix, reappear and live again.—HELMER.

I am not afraid of God's providences. Not afraid they will ever overthrow grace. Not afraid of man. And if it pleases God to develop new truths, to make larger disclosures, to give higher revelations of moral life, to open spheres for purer and nobler experiences: —these things are to be ours. And, as from the beginning, we have had solid truth that served the cause of religion, so we shall have solid truth that shall serve the cause of religion to the end.—BEECHER.

Therefore will not we fear though the earth be removed, and though the mountains be carried into the midst of the sea.

> ' And he in mercy loving,
>   Through weariness of years,
> Was kept unto the proving
>   Of hopes that knew not fears.
> In him when others faltered
>   Before the storm that blew,
> His mighty soul unaltered
>   By error's specious view:
>   Stormed in vain,
>   With no strain.
> Stood up unmoved and true.'

There is nothing nobler than faith, unwavering and unchanging in to-morrow and next year; in the unattempted, the untried, the unborn: the inherent, and unconquerable belief that our work, however humble and lowly, will, if earnest, result in good, and bring forth fruit acceptable in the eyes of the universal Father who sees the smallest flower bloom,

> ' And from the acorn rears the oak.'—FROTINGHAM.

30. *Where is the promise of his coming?*

> When shall these gloomy shadows be withdrawn
> And on us burst the effulgence of the dawn ?
> The bright, immortal morn ?—TARBOX.

> E'en now o'er the mountain it seems to me
> That a streak of gray appears :
> My God ! can it be that I see aright ?
> Can it be that the morning nears ?—J. A. S.

> 'It is coming sure and onward !
> Coming from the realms of day !
> While the spirit looking sunward,
> Like an eagle sees the ray.

> When the words of love shall waken
> World-wide fires in hearts of men;
> When the spirit shall be shaken.
> Till it finds its God again.'

God is the spring of pure being: separated from him by ignorance or false views, by conscious guilt, distrust or enmity, the soul carries in it the seeds of death, and in order to live, it must be restored to God, and God must be restored to its knowledge, confidence, and love.—YOUNG.

INDEX.